Everett W. Fish

The Egyptian Pyramids

An analysis of a great mystery

Everett W. Fish

The Egyptian Pyramids
An analysis of a great mystery

ISBN/EAN: 9783337239985

Printed in Europe, USA, Canada, Australia, Japan

Cover: Foto ©ninafisch / pixelio.de

More available books at **www.hansebooks.com**

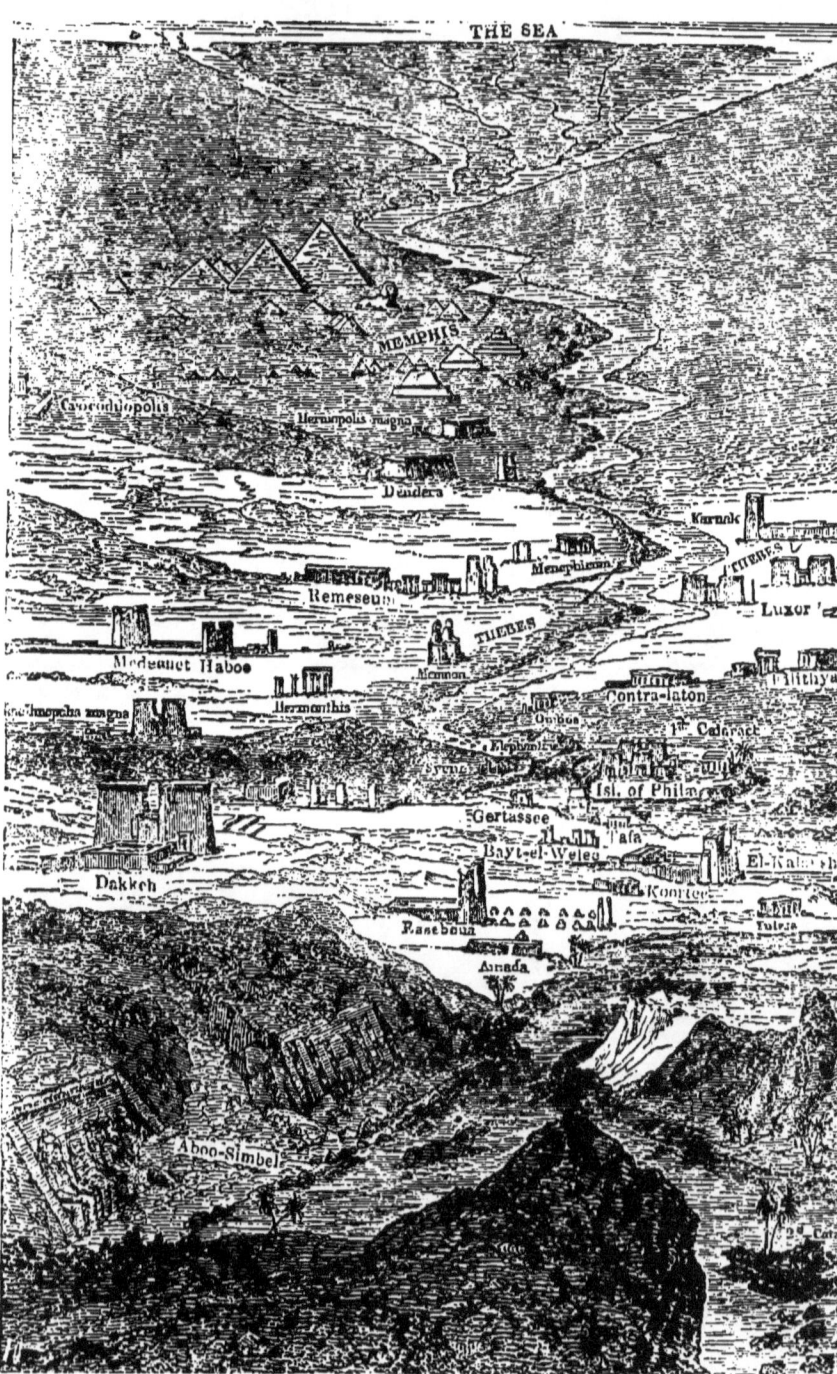

THE
EGYPTIAN ∴ PYRAMIDS:

AN ANALYSIS OF
A GREAT MYSTERY.

BY EVERETT W. FISH, M.D.

CHICAGO:
C. H. JONES & CO., 188 MONROE STREET.
1880.

Registered with the Librarian at Washington, D. C., Jan. 1880.

TO

Adnah Knight Frain, M.D.,

AN EARNEST STUDENT, IN ART AND SCIENCE,

Whose good opinion is valued more than the acclamation of the throng,

Is this Imperfect Token Inscribed.

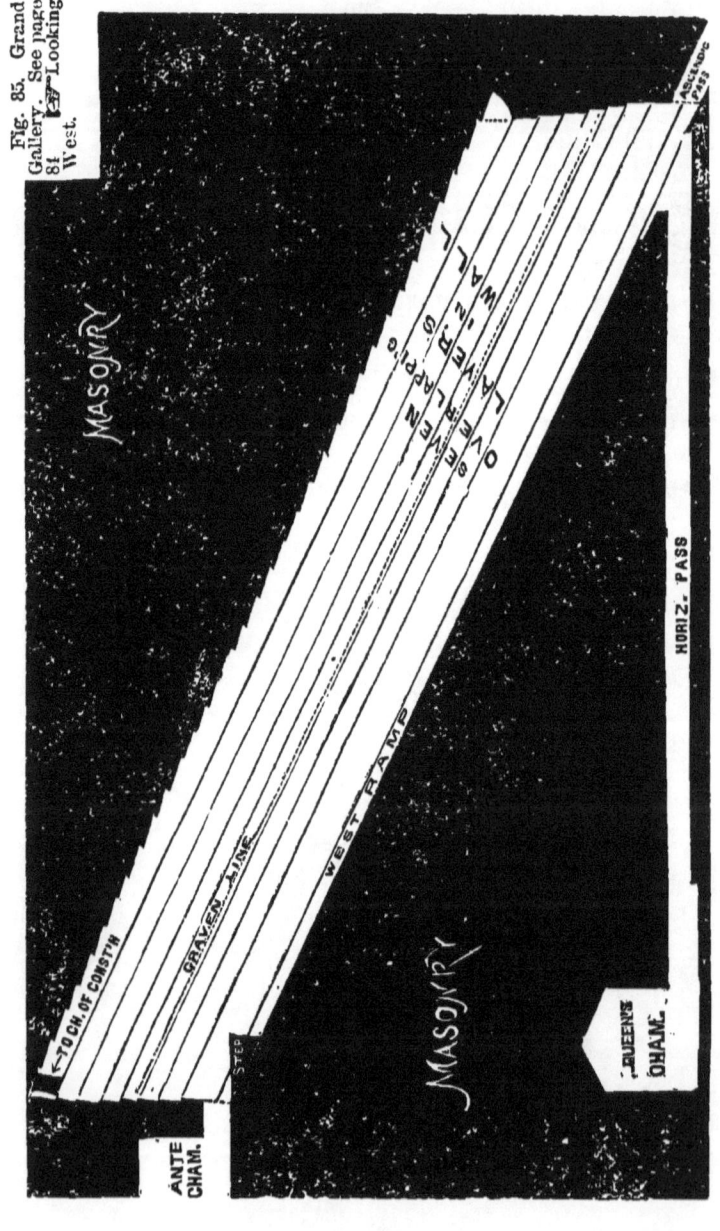

Fig. 85. Grand Gallery. See page 84. ☞ Looking West.

PREFACE.

SINCE this work was undertaken, with the view of presenting a purely scientific essay on the Pyramids, its plan has been materially changed. The range of study, necessary to develop the scientific features, has inwoven many religious coincidences, complicating the mystery of their origin, which it would be folly to cast aside.

It is not a proposition to be sneered at by the most inveterate theomachist, that the design, origin, and destiny of the Great Pyramid are theistic, although reasonably subject to negative criticism. Nor, though fashionable with most modern writers of materialistic views, does it comport with good sense and justice to underrate coincidences, which, as evidences, are opposed to our own views. But they should rather be weighed, value for value, with physical testimony; for the day has not yet come when we can either dogmatically negate the direct government of a spiritual essence, or demolish with rare *mepris* the intellectual giants, whose minds, (as broad and untrammeled as our own), have found "reason" in a divinity, and "common sense" in a revelation.

When the bases fall from the physical deductions of Kepler, Bacon, Newton, Napier, and an array of minds breaking from the shackles of past schools of thought to inaugurate new systems, but still beholding a God in the universe, then we may conclude that our views of theism and cosmogony are alone up to the level of philosophy, and consign theirs to neglect.

Prof. Piazzi Smyth may be too sanguine and over-positive in the application of Siriadic symbolisms; but the Scotchman's ken for theosophic mystery is a better guide to truth than the flippant pen of Jas. Bonwick, F. R. G. S. (London), in whose recent work there is a radical excision of such interpretations. However difficult of belief, a justly balanced mind will decide—not upon the capacity of the popular will for unbelief—but upon the intrinsic value of the evidences, in minds in which there is not a highly developed antagonism. Thus we ask the reader, even the most inveterate iconoclast, to read and study—under the influence of the broad principles of Baconian Philosophy.

CHICAGO, ILL., U. S. A.,
22 Ogden Ave.

In justice to a large body of Pyramid students who have been longer in the field than the writer, we caution the reader against giving too much weight to our opinion where it conflicts with others. The object of the work is to bring a grand subject before the masses, rather than discuss doubtful topics.

The orthography of Anglicized Egyptian words is exceedingly unsettled. For instance, the word Ghizeh may be spelled in twenty different ways

There will shortly appear more complete works upon Pyramid symbols, and hence we have left a more elaborate analysis to those who are more competent.

INTRODUCTION.

No problem of the present age so fully deserves the title— "A GREAT MYSTERY," as the origin and interpretation of the Egyptian Pyramids. Even the discovery of the key to the hieroglyphs, so profusely traced over the innumerable monuments, has left us in deeper darkness than before. For, as will be hereafter noted, in that land so pictured over with a stone literature, the Great Pyramid alone, amid the graven structures, was preserved pure and free from the idolatrous chisel.

Like the city of Damascus, this stupendous monument has witnessed the rise, zenith, and decay of empires whose armies have trodden the known world. But unlike this aged city, whose obscurity was often its safety, the Great Pyramid has been pre-eminent among its fellows in all ages — ever sleeping, yet unspeakably grand in the intensity of its slumber. Wonderful sleep! To wake, perchance— in this age — to an instant conflict with the progressive thought of four thousand years —— and then, probably, to triumph!

It has no humanly-written history. So far as known, its history is the translation of the singular symbols within itself,— without letter or language to speak in a living tongue. It has few traditions, no historian. The name of the builder is unknown. The era of its erection is a battle-ground 6000 years in extent. Its object is the giddy whim of some fifty different historians, whose interpretations vary with the weathercock. It was grey with the noons and nights of at least 600 years when the Pentateuch was written; it was as ancient to Moses as the Norman Conquest of England is to D'Israeli to-day. Undisturbed by earthquake, it will continue the monarch of monuments when the modern obelisk has wasted away, forgetting its own history, and trodden by the feet of a new race.

Modern science is struggling with a new element in this Pyramid. In dumb silence, it yet speaks of a wisdom so profound that the humbled disciples of Newton and Herchel shrink from it in surprise and wonder.

Very recently the freshly turned sod of Assyrian mounds gave us the most ancient landmarks of the human family, still leaving the great kingdoms of Iran and Bactria, to the northeast, involved in tradition; but in these later days the Coptic races in Ægypta, (either as subject or dominant people), throw a shadow athwart the history of the ancient world which involves all chronology and science in a tangled maze. Its dates, dynasties, fragments of history, traditions and hieroglyphics are all too snarled and discordant to throw certain light on the monuments from which its annals are derived.

This monument is peculiar. It strikes the architect as a structure built to defy the wrath of storms the wear of ages, and the hunger of fire. Nor is it strange that the student, who has soberly worked his way through Zend philosophy, Trojan relics, or the earliest twilight of Attic civilization, should rise into a higher enthusiasm when viewing this "Stone Age, " representing the most profound triumphs of human thought.

It was a new idea to the world, and its design is not yet delivered from the womb of stone, though modern doctors themselves appear in travail.

It is strange in all things.

It becomes in the earliest list the first and foremost of the seven wonders.

Whatever it may have cost to build, to destroy it would absorb the wealth of nations.

It is larger than any building or structure ever planted on earth's bosom. It is a higher pinnacle, if such proportions can be called a pinnacle, than the slender summit of the proudest temple ever built.

Its workmanship, in the interior passages, is the finest ever seen; yet amid the coarsest and rudest forms. A fine scroll and joint on some white temple front excites no wonder, but a joint of microscopic fineness between two mighty, granitic rocks, in a dark and narrow passage, amid huge forms of primitive material, is past all reason—beyond comprehension.

The Great Pyramid is different from those imitations built soon after, even in its mysterious aspects. For while their builders followed the pattern, in shape and proximate size—yet, not knowing ALL the secrets of the overshadowing pile, they fill no channel of advanced symbolism.

But more mysterious than its exterior majesty, or interior symbolisms, is the fact—fairly established—that as soon as it was completed it was sealed up by a massive coating of limestone so that no man penetrated its interior for thousands of years—not until man's cupidity led him to force an entrance by chisel, fire, and vinegar, in search for hidden treasures.

To day this mighty child of antiquity is ragged and battered. Its beautiful casing has built more modern palaces, and its interior is robbed of much of its beauty and finish. The outside has been despoiled by the Arab—but the inside by the civilized barbarians who whack at every relic of the past with a tourist's hammer. But while they may hack away its polished walls and batter down the exquisite coffer in the King's Chamber, there is one source of satisfaction—they cannot, in ages, sensibly reduce its immense mass.

ANALYSIS.

THERE are so many singular deductions and coincidences derived from the Great Pyramid, that we have classed them somewhat as follows, to render their study more clear and satisfactory:—

FIRST.

That the Pyramid is found to be an historical tablet, as it were; constructed to give by a series of measurements the great epochs of the past. Not only of the past, but also premising (prophetic) great historical and cosmical changes in the future.

SECOND.

That it represents many astronomical facts and phases, giving data in that science that would be impossible were the builder ignorant of the shape of the earth, its size, density, weight, and position among the planets. It is claimed that it gives, more correctly than "human agencies" of this advanced era, the distance of the sun, etc. Its correct orientation also presents curious questions.

THIRD.

That the cosmical relations of the earth are used to elaborate a system of universal weights and measures based on a system lately attempted by the French nation, but vastly superior to the French method from a mathematical standpoint, as now recognized by scientists—in fact being the only method of securing the desired object mathematically correct. That these measures were also the same as the "sacred" measure units of the Hebrews, and the present scale in use by the Anglo-Saxons.

FOURTH.

That it represents great mathematical problems, which have puzzled great minds in all ages, but which are as nearly solved in the Pyramid as an infinite progression will allow. This is instanced in the Quadrature of the Circle.

It also solves the physical problem of securing unalterable temperature for certain scientific questions—as the measurement of mass attraction, and the preservation of length standards.

FIFTH.

That divisions of time are not only rightly indicated by months and years, but the different kind of months is represented, and the fractional day provided for by "leap years" and correct cycles.

SIXTH.

It is urged strongly by many that this Pyramid is a part of the Hebraic theosophy and the logos; that thus it prophesied Christ and promises His future kingdom. Also that the Bible frequently refers to it as a direct work from God's hand—and especially as a testimony and a witness for some modern epoch—"near the end"—when it should be no longer a dead monument, but a "lively oracle." In regard to this branch of the subject we can scarcely see the wonderful things which many discover, but the subject has been as strongly developed as any other class of evidences, and we leave the student to form his own opinions.

SEVENTH.

It either designedly, or by coincidence, represents an unnumbered array of minor problems, astonishing, if not convincing of a more than human agency concerned in the erection. As observed, these may be coincidences, but, if so, they are the most remarkable that an elastic mind can entertain.

These propositions may not embrace all the "curiosities" attached to our wonderful subject. For taken in connection with the unreasonable snarl and tangle in its history; the unexplainable sealing from human sight of its interior; the quite well known views of Egypt's ancient astronomers; the before-mentioned absence of the hieroglyphics; the magnitude of its dimensions and the partial failure of the "Tomb theory"—and the Pyramid of Gizeh stands out upon the frontier of the desert as the most wonderful Mystery of the age, and the most sublime landmark in the history of man.

THE VALUE OF THE EVIDENCE.

ANCIENT Egypt promises to furnish modern Christendom with material for an extended discussion; and it is quite possible that the field of religious investigation will for a time be transferred from the Jordan to the Nile.

In this critical day, people of broad views and general intelligence are not convinced, even of an exalted truth, by a single train of evidences. It is only by the gradual modifications of the channels of thought that propositions in social, moral or æsthetic life acquire a general acceptance.

The purpose of this little work is to present the question in such a manner that the mind may grasp the facts and judge them as we judge general history, without warp or bias. Many deductions seem unphilosophical to the writer, yet it is no more than fair to give them in their strongest light, lest we fail to do justice to those whose studies have given them a right to full hearing.

A great objection to the mathematical and chronological testimony of the Pyramid, as evidence, is, that any given structure, having proportions, halls, chambers, and angles, may be so manipulated as to yield equally wonderful results. In this way a member of the British Scientific Association reviewed Prof. Piazzi Smyth's work on the Pyramid, ridiculing the propositions and deductions of the learned astronomer. Calling for the tri-cornered hat of an auditor, he proceeded to measure it—and to the

---

*It was doubtless the spirit in which the Pyramid labors of Prof. Smyth were received that led to his separation from the Royal Society, even if it were not the d rect cause. However, his withdrawal, referred to on the next page, was not due solely to resentment at this indiscreet exhibition before a body of scientists,

sport of the society, deduced therefrom some exact mathematical data.

To the credit of the Professor be it said, he indignantly withdrew from membership in the body. For such was not the place, nor hour, to treat flippantly and with sneer a great problem which has since drawn into its discussion the best minds of the scientific world; and which affects the entire field of intellectual and religious development in a startling degree.

It may be said of this member, that his sarcasm was lost on the world when it was found that his figures on the "hat" had been prepared before hand, and his deductions "cut and dried." The reader will recognize, of course, that any one may construct a building, or plan a hat, with dimensions to fit any given set of past dates or arithmetical proportions. But the question of pyramidical evidence goes deeper than this. It is required:

1st. That the structure presents data of which the "artist" is quite ignorant, or which are so advanced beyond his own age as to be entirely incomprehensible to his fellow-beings—e. g.: The rotundity of the earth, distance of the planets, and various other cosmical measures, meridians, etc.

A just estimation of the past not only pronounces the Egyptians ignorant of these things, —*ignorance crasse*— but every people on earth were thus ignorant; and farther, such relative science as there was, taught a cosmogony directly the reverse of Pyramid science.*

2d. The structure must not only give past data, but it must either by design or "coincidence" represent future events. These coincidental or prophetic symbols must

---

*The Hipparchian and Ptolemaic systems of astronomy represent the leading ideas of advanced thought for a thousand years B. C. Before this the Egyptians were even unable to establish a cycle.

refer only to those events which modify universal history. In the Pyramid we have this illustrated in the founding of the Hebrew nation, whose history and theocratic nature have modified every subsequent political power on earth. The Exodus, and the Birth of Christ, are also among the coincidences.

3d. The structure must not only give recognition to mathematical propositions, but it must attempt the solution of profound problems which have harassed the student for ages.

Whether the above conditions are fairly credited to the Pyramid will remain an open question, until time reveals its purposes.

As a test, however, of the position taken by the member of the British Association, we present the student with the figure on page 157. (Figure 83.) It is the plan of a structure. It is required that from its dimensions, or the manipulation of dimensions by indicated factors, a list of chronological or mathematical data is to be deduced, relating to any science or special line of history. Nor is it required that future events be figured out! With the view of assisting the student, a certain dimension has been made to represent, even to the one ten-thousandth of an inch, an important era in history. This is the period in Roman History from the founding of the city to the death of Julius Cæsar.

The only requirements would be, (a), That the events, etc., shall be of primary importance in the line of history or science represented; and (b), that coincidences shall coincide to .01 of a unit. Also, (c), that no factor shall be used that is not related either to the history or to the structure.

Few readers will realize the injustice done to the School

who are translating the symbolism of the Pyramid, in this proposition. For the most remarkable coincidences of the Great Monument are not riddles to be solved by "midnight oil," or "child-birth pain," but are startling in their distinctness. It is quite possible that they are coincidences only; it is quite possible they are not! At all events they are readily discovered.

For a further development of the nature of the evidence, let us wander from the cold, abstract study of stone to a warmer illustration, which, while less logical from its coloring, appeals more directly to the common-sense:

A teacher in Ancient History, to divide off the ages into convenient epochs, made use of certain Biblical dates. Not that all of them were absolute, but that they were relatively convenient.

Suppose that such a teacher were to travel in a strange land, and receive hospitality at the hands of some recluse or iconoclast, the threshold of whose gate has never before been passed by man. He enters a broad avenue. He finds before him a pathway lined with rare flowers, graceful foliage and curious exotics. The Old Man leads the traveler towards the distant mansion. Of a sudden he notices unique stakes set in the ground, and on them, painted figures.* Little attention is paid to this at first. But soon a smile appears on the teacher's face, as he recognizes an old friend on one of these stakes—number 2349, (supposed date of the Flood—close of the first epoch in his history class). No other idea is entertained, however, than that these figures are some common place plan of a half-crazed fossil of a gardener. But the stranger's eyes open wider, when, about a hundred feet farther on, he meets another old friend in the number 2247; (given by some as the

---

*Figures are given as a stranger would have no occasion to apply a measuring line to these divisions of the garden.

date of the "Dispersion"). Again the beauty of the grounds attracts his attention, when stranger things appear. First a familiar number in small figures, 1729, which is followed closely by another in bold characters, 1491. (Date of the "Exodus," and formation of the Hebrew nation). "Surely," he soliloquized, "this old man's reputation belies him. There is some significance in all this, especially if some peculiar change in the garden appear about 1500 feet further on, symbolizing the Christian era." Who can judge of the surprise and wonder when at just such a distance the pathway abruptly opened upon a most magnificent fountain! And a few hundred feet beyond, another familiar date appears on a "time post"—(the date of the Hegira of Mahomet), and the gate of the castle door is reached some 1881 feet from the fountain. But the wonder does not cease here. All through that castle—every where—are numbers and measures which the wanderer had made familiar to his class! In utter amazement, he turns to his rough, weather-beaten guide, and asks him whence all this intricate knowledge of the past and prophecy of the future? The old man turns to his questioner, and with eyes burning with mysterious fire, replies, "Stranger, let it still remain, as it has been, a mystery! When the time comes thou shalt know." The traveler answers—" It is no mystery—it is all a coincidence."

We will strip this scene of its fancy, its flowers, its dreamery, and we have the cold facts of that mighty structure whose study is the mystery of the age! Let us enter the portal, behold the testimony upon which to answer the question—"Was it built as a history in rock—with wisdom symbolized in every feature?—or the chance creation of some ancient king whose bones have disappeared from their grand mausoleum?

THE EARLY HISTORY OF EGYPT.

THE early history of the earliest nation would naturally be involved in doubt and uncertainty. But the history of Egypt is so entangled—not in tradition alone, but in conflicting records—that no satisfactory chronology can be deduced from them. The following analysis is given in the vain hope that it may approach the truth. In this chronology a small amount of the geological evidence is given more value than almost any other ancient testimony.

Egypt as a whole, occupies the northeastern corner of Africa. On the west it is partially protected from the encroaching desert sands by the Libyan mountains. On the east it has been defended from the warlike Ishmaelite and desert influences of Arabia, by the Red Sea. Its remarkable fertility is annually reinforced by the phenomenal inundations of the River Nile.

Egypt, provincially, has in the far past been cut up into various provinces and city governments, each of which at times were independent kingdoms. Of old, the whole valley, from the cataract to the sea, was divided into three sections of uncertain boundary. The Northern, including the fertile delta, was known as Bahara, in which were at different times several prominent kingdoms and cities: Memphis, in ancient times, and Alexandria in more modern, have been the most important. Heracleopolis was also the seat of a kingdom. Xois, in the delta, a city of a powerful priesthood, for several dynasties maintained an independent government. The southern section is called the "Said," the "Thebais," or "Thebaid," a district once having Thebes for its populous and powerful capital. The Greek name of Thebes was Diospolis and her kings are frequently called Diospolitan. Between Said and Bahara was the region of Vostani. The earliest kingdom in Egypt was that of "This," in the southern portion which antedated Thebes. Its kings were known as Thinites. The Elephantine kings were also prominent and powerful at an early age Map on p. 151.

The most complete sources of our information regarding the history of this ancient territory are the hieroglyphics, or stone pictures on the monuments. Perhaps, if all the monuments were preserved, they might be deciphered correctly and harmoniously. Unfortunately such is not the case. Herodotus visited Egypt about the 5th century B. C. (484), and wrote a history of the country. The Egyptian priests gave him much information, but he being unable to translate the hieroglyphics to any great extent,—and his record being largely mythical, it is not credible in all its statements. The Bible also gives many interesting notes, all of which have been corroborated by the Egyptian records. An exceedingly valuable work was produced in the 3d century B. C., by Manetho, high-priest of Heliopolis, giving the names of 30 dynasties of kings, from the founder of Thebes to the times of Darius II. But unfortunately the history of Manetho has been lost, and we only have distorted portions in the works of subsequent writers.

Among these are Eratosthenes, (276 B. C.); Julius Africanus, (300 B. C.); Diodorus, (60 B. C.); Strabo, (A. D.), and Syncellus (800 A. D.).

There was also the Turin Tablet, a papyrus scroll, of ancient date, having an astronomical system of chronology, but it has become almost or quite illegible. On the temple at Abydos, (This), there were certain lists of kings, which are of great use to us.

But there is inextricable confusion, notwithstanding the varied sources of information. Even the Biblical record is of little use, for there is no settled system of chronology to which the student can anchor. The short chrono'ogy, giving the Flood at 2349, B. C., (D∴ Usher's) is usually adopted; but it is radically opposed to all other systems, and the Samaritan and Alexandrian (Septuagint) versions place it at least 1300 years earlier.

THE HIEROGLYPHICS.

Until the close of the last century, the picture writing of the Egyptians remained untranslated. In 1799 there was discovered at Roseta, a stone tablet, upon which was engraved a trilingual key to these singular symbols. The figures of this "Sacred writing" were translated into the Greek and enchorial or demotic alphabets. It was engraven B. C. 200, but the indifference of the brilliant School of Philosophy at Alexandria not only permitted hieroglyphics to cease without papyrus works on the subject— but allowed this one tablet to be forgotten for 2000 years.

The stone inscriptions were the earliest types of written language. In word representation, though not in morphology, they resemble Chinese syllabicism. Certain forms, either natural or artificial, became associated with certain ideas—sometimes relative, sometimes cognate—and were henceforth used to represent them. In the course of years, the idea character became contracted to a word or syllable.

The next step was the representation of a sound instead of a syllable, although the word and syllable forms were never entirely supplanted.

Thus, Osiris, a demi-god, was hieroglyphed with two syllabic characters, *Os* and *Iri*, (Fig. 2). On the other hand Labaris, a king of This, had both syllabic and sound characters, L, A, O, B, Ra, (Fig. 2.).

Fig. 2. Another modification followed the development of sound characters.

It was the simplification of the character itself. Owing to the extreme veneration of the Egyptians for their "sacred writing," this improvement is scarcely recognized in the Nile Valley. Hieroglyphs formed after the Advent much resembled those of the early ages of Karnac and Luxor. But the neighboring nations, Hebrews, Greeks, Syro-Phœnicians, and the Edomites, probably through the necessities of commerce, profited by the picture "ideation," and developed alphabets.* The fact is, that European literature is the offspring of the Egyptian monuments. Fig. 5 gives a scheme for the origin of the Hebrew characters, and Fig. 4 one for the Greek, through Phœnicia. The engravings closely follow Sharpe. The transformation into Hebrew characters must have been very ancient or it may have been through Edom's civilization. Of course it will be understood that Egypt antedates Edom at least a thousand years.

Fig. 3.

Through Egypt came science, philosophy, and even liter-

---

*According to Sir Isaac Newton letters originated, not in Phœnicia, but in Edom, among the Troglodytes, or dwellers in the magnificent cave- or cliff-palaces of Petrea. Doubtless the descendants of Cush and Ham in Egypt, and of Esau in Edom both drew their earliest "ideations" from a common source, many centuries before Assyria had a literature. Edom offered incense to art, and faded; Egypt changed not, and her history dwells eternally in her monuments.

EARLY HISTORY OF EGYPT.

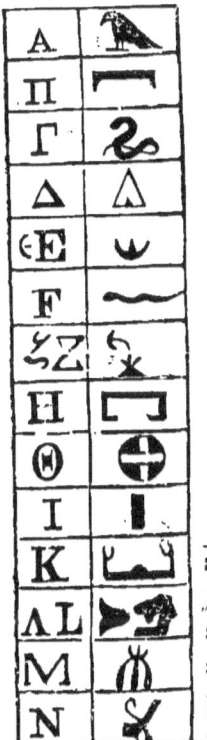

Fig. 4. Origin of Greek characters.

ature to Europe. While one age gave *form* to sound, the glorious Alexandrian epoch gave life and form to thought, and *invention* to science. One beautiful pillar is wanting in the grand vestibule of Egypt's history—Art! But had Egypt developed art, or had the æsthetic supplanted the indestructible, then those heavy, sombre, fadeless records, in tomb and temple, pyramid and obelisk, would have crumbled on papyrus rolls, or been burned out by the torch of despot and fanatic—buried in common with the history of Iran and Edom. There is a mystery in the peculiar nature of Coptic development.

THE TIMES OF MENES.

From a careful study of the traditions of Egypt and other nations, during the 1000 years preceding the carliest reliable dates, it is barely possible to locate a few prominent events. But even then the confirmation of the geological evidence, soon referred to, is necessary to make these proximate dates at all trustworthy. It is during this uncertain epoch that the Great Pyramid was built.

The era of the Rise of Thebes to the rank of a powerful city is an important landmark. This especially turns upon the fall of the kingdom of the city of This, (or Abydos), when the throne of Upper Egypt was removed to the new and populous city of Thebes. Equally significant of the rise of the new power was the Theban conquest of Memphis, by Menes. This event, as well as the establishment of the Sun-god Amun-Ra, (Fig. 6), and the founding of the memorial temples of Karnak and Luxor, peer indistinctly through the misty history of this era.

Menes was possibly a mythical person. He was undoubtedly the same as the Menu of the Hindus, and the Minos of the Greeks. It is very remarkable that the tradition of the great Turanian, Arian, and the

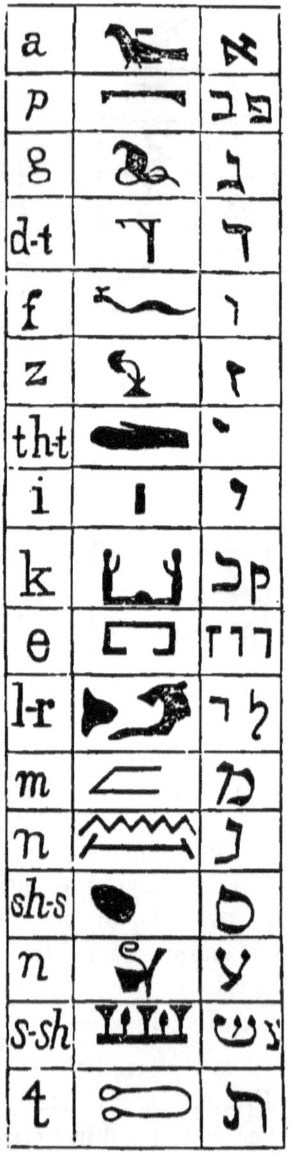

Fig. 5. Origin of Hebrew letters.

Hamitic races, great branches of the common origin of the human family, should thus converge to one common head, a mighty conqueror—and a wise statesman.

Menes was supposed, by Heroditus, to have ruled over Egypt 2000 B. C.; but his history is mixed with Hellenic traditions, and many such statements must be taken with due allowance. It is reasonably certain that Abraham migrated to Egypt about 1900 B. C., at which time Thebes was past her early glory, having been at least once conquered by Memphis. It is generally admitted that Menes founded the city.

An analysis of the dynasties preceding that during which Abraham appeared at Memphis, has resulted in a few chronologists placing the founding of Thebes at 1000 years before that event, or 2900 B. C. This conclusion is fortified by a careful examination of the alluvial deposits of the River Nile, by its never failing annual overflow.

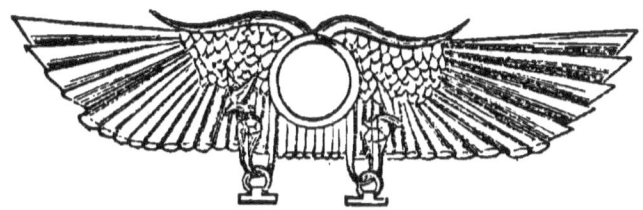

Fig. 6. Amun-Ra, the Sun-God.

We think this resource for historical research has been slighted by Egyptologists, although the French Academicians did much to develop the subject.

It has been shown that the addition to the soil every one hundred years amounts to nearly five inches.* Over

---
*According to certain other explorations it was put at from 3 to 4 inches but it was in a location where the body of overflow was less than at Karnac and Luxor.

the foundation platforms of the most ancient Theban temples there is a deposit of over nineteen feet. By these centennial strata it is estimated that the city was founded or greatly enlarged from 2800 to 3000 B. C. The enlargement can be justly assigned to the close of the Thinite dynasties, and consolidation of Egypt under Menes. The agreement of different alluvial examinations, with each other and with certain other evidences, gives great probability to our deductions; and it is hoped they will receive farther examination.

Manetho, though not wholly at variance, does not fully warrant these conclusions. Unfortunately we get his history percolated through half-a-dozen later writers. Thus, he says Menes reigned at "This," over a kingdom stretching from Lycopolis unto Tentyra, building the city of Thebes during his reign; and seventeen Thinite kings followed before the removal of the throne to Thebes. Then we have from 500 to 700 years of unbroken reigns recorded by the monuments.

The Greek student will not fail to discover Grecian footprints in this statement. It might make the record of less weight to remind the reader that Attic civilization dawned some twenty-five hundred years after the times of Menes.

MEMPHIS.

The above record of the reign of 17 Thinite kings, if correct, added to the 600 years of Theban supremacy, brings us to a period when the latter kingdom succumbed to Memphis. And this conquest of Thebes was by a foreign invader, whose first achievement was to win, by force or strategy, the throne of Memphis. His name was Cheops, (Fig. 7), and he doubtless built the Great Pyramid of Ghizeh. Manetho has no dynasty which includes Cheops, (4th dynasty), and ascribes the Great Pyramid to Suphis, of the 6th. At the time of this supremacy of Memphis, (4th) Manetho puts in king Timaus, thus: "We had formerly a king, Timaus. In his time it came to pass, I know not how, that the Deity was displeased with us, and there came up from the East, in a strange manner, men of an ignoble race, who had the confidence to invade our country and easily subdue it by their power, without a battle. And when they had *our rulers in their hands*, they demolished the temples of the Gods."

Fig. 7. Cheops, Suphis, Chemmis, or Chofo. Sometimes Shafre.

Fig. 8. Sen-Suphis, Noum Chofo, Chephren. Brother of Cheops.

Note the italics! The Egyptian priest never admitted a direct conquest. We have two indications in this expression: That the conquest was a very strange one, and that the native Egyptians were not the "Yoingees," soon referred to, for the latter were but recently driven from home. However, the Hindu race may have been the invaders.

Here is a race that conquers by intelligence. The Egyptian priest, Manetho, who through hatred, never mentions Cheop's name, places the invasion at the time noted for the pyramid builders, and also for the conquest of the city of Thebes. We will note that Cheop's name is omitted, and also the name of the king of the "ignoble race." This singular conquest is corroborated by a closely parallel Hindoo tradition, to which reference will again be made. Dr. Seiss, in the "Miracle in Stone," and others, consider Timaus as the Chemmis of Diodorus, the Cheops of Heroditus, Chufu or Shofo of the monuments.

Then of course he was himself the Suphis of Manetho,—a not very plausible proposition, as two or three dynasties intervened, according to the chronicler of both. The testimony does not show that Cheops or Suphis ever was conquered. On the other hand he was a mighty conqueror himself; he and his successor, Sensuphis, or Chephren, having spread their kingdom over all Egypt and Sinaitic Arabia. Suphis reigned 63 years, and is himself represented as destroying the temples and the Gods. Cheops is always spoken of as alien to Coptic interests. Yet Mr. Bonwick says he was an Egyptian, and of an Egyptian dynasty, apparently a very bold assertion. Manetho avoids the mention of his name, and the Egyptian priests so hated him that they mentioned his name in scorn, and ascribed the building of the Pyramid to one of his shepherds, as in derision.* Again, after Timaus, Manetho leaves an unsatisfactory record from the 3d or 4th dynasty till the 6th. We can see in Timaus the last of the 3d dynasty of priestly kings, and in Cheops, an invader and the first of the Hycsos. Heroditus states: "(128). The Egyptians so detest the memory of these [the two first—Cheops and Cephren] that they do not much like even to mention their names, hence they commonly call the pyramids [the Great and the 2d] after Philition [or Philitis] a shepherd, who at that time fed his flocks about the place."

Now follow this up with what Manetho says of the conquerors of Timaus:—

"All this invading nation was styled Hycsos, that is 'Shepherd Kings;' for the first syllable, 'Hyc' in sacred dialect denotes a king; and 'sos' signifies a shepherd, but this only according *to the vulgar tongue.* And of these is compounded the term Hycsos; some say they were Arabians,"

---

*And yet the Egyptians were none of them Shepherds—evidence that Cheops was not an Egyptian.

It is singular that so able a man as Dr. Seiss, and his confreres, does not recognize the import of these excerpts.

Not only does it imply that Cheops and his followers were the shepherd conquerors, but it inadvertently gives ample testimony, which is worth more than the inference drawn from the statement:—

The Egyptians were not shepherds. They hated the avocation. Thus, while Heroditus, in speaking of Cheops gives us a picture of a shepherd on Pyramid hill, Manetho, (referring to the conqueror of Timaus) gives the derivation of hyksos in which the word "sos," is relegated with pointed scorn, to the "vulgar tongue." The word "shepherd" was alien to them. Cheops was the Pyramid builder and king of the shepherd race.

The successor of Cheops was the Cephren of Heroditus and Diodorus; Suphis II or Sen-suphis, ("Sen" meaning brother), of Manetho; and the Noum- or Non-Shofo of Egyptologists. Cartouche, or hieroglyph in Fig. 8.

The next Memphite king was Mencheres of Manetho, and the Moscherus, and Menkere of others. These three kings are intimately connected with the history of the three Pyramids of Ghizeh. It is generally considered that they constituted an epoch in Egyptian history, during which foreign influence prevailed throughout the valley, modifying Egyptian customs, intelligence, and religion. It is also recorded that they finally adopted the gods of the native races, and hence remained in power several centuries, and were then driven out intact, being neither destroyed, nor conquered to servitude.

THEBAN PONTIFF-KINGS.

At this time Thebes appears to partially throw off the Memphite yoke under a succession of native kings. There is great doubt, however, as to the relations these priest-kings bore to the Memphite monarchs, who are supposed to have been the shepherd kings: Osirtesen I, (Fig. 9), ascended the Theban throne, and it is said, erected those older and grander buildings which now mark the ruins of his capital. This seems unreasonable, however, when we reflect that Thebes had been a mighty city nearly ten centuries before, and at least 500 years before the silence of the wilderness was broken by the builders of Babylon!

Fig. 9. Osirt-sen I. Title over first oval is "Sot-Nout," or King over Upper and Lower Egypt. Title over the second is "Sera," Son of the Sun. The first oval reads, "Ho-ke-ra," Ra being read last. Second oval reads O-S-R-T-S-N.

Fig. 10. Mesphra-Thothmosis. Characters read, in second oval, Mes-(anvil) [ph]Ita-Thoth (character under fowl)-M S-S. Comparison with Figs. 4 and 5 will assist translation.

Wilkinson puts the reign of Osirtesen at about the time of Joseph's arrival at Memphis, or 1706, B. C., which we are compelled to regard as an error. Sharpe places Osirtesen about 1750 also, but Joseph about 200 years later, under Mesphra-Thothmosis, (Fig. 10), who expelled the shepherd kings.

Thebes, before the time of Osirtesen, had extended her conquests from beyond Libya to the Indus, had gone into decline, been conquered by Memphis, and was now rising into new glory, possibly under the shadow and yoke of Memphis. It is quite probable that Osirtesen did extend

Karnak, rebuild Luxor, and restore the gods and shrines overthrown by the earlier conqueror of Timaus and of Thebes.

The immediate predecessor of Osirtesen I seems to have been Amunmai Thori, (Fig. 11), who is supposed to have resisted or conquered Memphis. The successors of Osirtesen, of whom little is known, appear as Noubkouri, or Amunmai Thori II (Fig 12), Meshophra, or Osirtesen II

Fig. 11. Amunmai Thori. Characters in second oval A-M-N-M-T-R. Also called A. Ch(k)ori, "Conqueror beloved by Amun."

Fig. 12. Amunmai Thori II, or Noubk(ch)ori.

(Fig 13), Meskora, or Osirtesen III (14), Queen Scemiophra (Fig 15). These names do not appear at all in the Memnon list at Thebes, but do appear on the Abydos tablet. As Abydos had been a powerful kingdom centuries before, it does not add much to the clearness of the record. It was during these reigns that Abraham appeared in lower Egypt, at Memphis, (1900 B. C.).

By some writers, the names just given as rulers of all Egypt are represented as merely High Priests. Either contemporaneously, or following these kings of equivocal power, Memphis was said to be again invaded by a foreign race, who held all Egypt under tribute. According to Manetho, they were Phœnicians, also called Hyksos or shepherd kings. There were six of them, Salatis, Beon,

A GREAT MYSTERY.

Apachnas, Apophis, Janias, and Asseth, (Sharpe), and were driven out by Chebros-Amosis, (Fig 16), the *successor of Queen Scemiophra!* If this is so, and Manetho states it, then the relative history of the Cheops and Salatis eras are

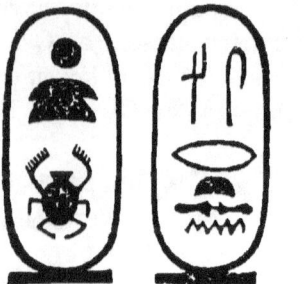 

Fig. 13. Ovals of Osirtesen II, or Meshophra.

Fig. 14. Ovals of Osirtesen III, or Meskora.

inextricably mixed, and the effort to place the successors of Mykera is hopeless, for Cheops and his successors in-

Fig.15. Queen Scemiophra, the last ruler of Thebes who submitted to the Hyksos invaders. (Manetho.)

Fig. 16. Chebros-Amosis, who expelled the Hyksos. As he was a direct successor of Osirtesen it confirms our opinion that the Cheopian and Salatian invasions, if not identical, were closely related.

Fig. 17. Chebros-Amosis II.

cluding the six foreigners just mentioned closed an era also closed at Thebes by the military success of Chebros-Amosis, who drove the foreigners out.

Then were the two epochs but one? The six foreign kings held Thebes, as did Cheops before, and hence the Theban rulers must have been high priests or governors—as one ancient historian suggests.

Again, while on this subject we give place to the following, which is of weight:— "The shepherd story [of the builders of the Pyramid] brings to mind the Hindoo narative of some early race of India, the Pali, who were a shepherd people, ancestors of the present aboriginal Bheels, succeeding once in conquering Egypt. Their stronghold, Abaris, is in sanskrit [a monotheistic race, we infer from this source] 'a shepherd;' Goshena is in sanskrit 'the land of shepherds.'—Jas. Bonwick, *Pyramid Facts and Fancies*.

The Bheels, if the tradition is true, were the Cheopian invaders, according to Bonwick. Yet an ancient writer has it that the same "Abaris" was a stronghold of the Phœni-

Fig. 18. Queen Nitocris.

Fig. 19. Thothmosis II.

cian (?) conquerors "who scourged Egypt for 100 years,' and were finally driven out by Chebros-Amosis—referring unquestionably to the Salatian dynasty. Sharpe puts it at about 1500 B. C., thus confounding them with the Hebrews, who—at this time—existed only in prophetic promises.

Again: "We read in the Hindu Paranas of a war between the gods and earthborn 'Yoingees.' The latter were vanquished and retreated to Egypt."—*Ibid.* Mr. Wilson, an eminent writer on the astronomy of the ancients is inclined to ascribe great intellectual power to the "Yoin-

Fig. 20. Amunophth I. Fig. 21. Thothmosis III.

gees" and believes them the pyramid builders of that age.

NATIVE KINGS.

The centre of government, after the expulsion of the last of shepherd kings, was at Thebes. Chebros-Amosis was followed by a son of same name, and next was Amunothph I, (Fig 20) who was worshipped quite as much as any of his predecessors.

Mespra-Thothmosis II (Fig. 19), enlarged the temples of Thebes and added to the glory of the kingdom. The monuments of this age are covered with inscriptions. It was a "golden age" of hieroglyphs. It was the era of the migration of Jacob to lower Egypt, and the ministry of Joseph at Memphis. Amun-Nitocris, (Fig. 18), wife of Mespra-Thothmosis II, was an ambitious woman whose influence was felt throughout the kingdom. An eminent writer tells us she united Thebes to her kingdom by diplomacy. As we supposed we were dealing with a Theban dynasty in Mespra-Thothmosis, this part of her prowess we do not understand.

A few years subsequent to the reign of Amun-Nitocris, under Amunophth II, son of Thothmosis III, the Exodus of the Israelites occurred. Having now reached a better foot-

Fig. 22. Amunophth II.

Fig. 23. Amunmai Thori III.

ing in chronology, we close the epoch. This scarcely understandable analysis of this doubtful period is given for the reason that the mystery of its history is a necessary part of the study of the Pyramid.

Many of our names have been in accord with Sharpe, with several variations however, and different deductions. Down to the reign of Queen Nitocris there were 12 kings of Thebes, agreeing essentially with Eratosthenes, the

Tablet of Abydos, and others. In confirmation of our belief in Chofo's or Cheops being a part of the first Hycsos invaders, Eratosthenes places him after Noubkori, or Amunmai II, at which time Thebes was under Memphite rule.

The following schedule of dynasties will conclude a chapter on the most conflicting history in human annals:

No. of DYN'TY.	KINGS IN "SAID," MOSTLY THEBAN.	KINGS IN "BAHARA," MOSTLY MEMPHITE.
	17 Thinite kings of Manetho. Exceedingly doubtful.	Nothing known.
1.	Menes, 2800 or 2900 B.C.	Priest-kings conquered by Menes.
2-3.	500 or 600 years of Theban kings.	Usually under Theban dominion.
4.	Conquered by Cheops the invader. Osirtesen and successors	Cheops conquers Timaus, 2200 B.C., and begins the Hyksos reigns.
12	Qu. Nitocris mentioned. Without reason. to Chebros-Amosis.	Cephren or Sensuphis. Menkere. The Salatian Hyksos kings. Hyksos expelled. About 1900 B.C.

ETHNOLOGY.

We have thus given as substantial a record of the earliest 1500 years of Egyptian history, as our pages and resources will admit.

This embraces the period from Menes to the departure of the Israelites, and, without a question, includes the Pyr-

EARLY HISTORY OF EGYPT. 39

amid era. Now let us take a view of the ethnological characters of the race or races at that time in the Nile valley.

There are many indications which point to Egypt as a field on which a great intellectual struggle transpired between two grand divisions of the human family,—the Mongol or Turanian, and the Semite or Aryo-Semitic. After a certain period elapses from the founding of Thebes

Fig. 24. Mongolian Type.   Fig. 25. Semitic Type.

we find the character of the people a well-developed Semitic type. But in the earliest ages, especially at Memphis, and always among her lower native castes, there is an equally well developed Mongolian, or at least Hamitic, expression. There are many indications that the earliest settlers of both Thebes and the Delta were Asiatics, while the glorious works of Morphology exhibited at Thebes a few centuries later, in which contour begins to supplant immensity, come in contact with the still unæsthetic culture of the lower Nile. Dr. Richardson says:—"Neither in their feature nor in their complexion have the Copts the smallest resemblance to the figures of the ancient Egyptian races as represented in the tombs at Thebes, or *in any other part of Egypt*,"—an unsupported assertion, that is quite too strong. However, in the earlier epoch, even in Thebes, the graven faces were those of the modern "fellah." (Fig 24). In the oldest paintings, at Thebes or Memphis, the female face was tinged with the Tartar yellow. The fact that they would not eat of flesh on religious grounds; that they abhorred the sea; that they wore the single lock of hair; also the shape of the upper maxilary; the worship of the bull, and many traditions, point strongly to a Hindoo origin.

But the change of facial and cranial type which soon occurred, points distinctly to an irruption into the Nile valley of a race of people differing from the native settlers. It constitutes apparently a new element in Siriad history. That the original inhabitants were not lacking in culture, nor intellect, is witnessed by the power Memphis developed before the first invasion. That the struggle between the two races was a silent contest extending through ages of internal intercourse, is undoubted. Still, Memphis, which first received the invading intellect, did not take so kindly to the change as Thebes, so that those sculptures representing the Semitic type, (see Fig 25), are generally found in the ruins of Upper Egypt. Egyptologists have not recognized this change of type sufficiently, as an historical element. Whether it was produced by the migration of a large tribe of nomads, or whether it was the earliest conquest by the shepherd kings, a race intellectually developed, with a monotheistic religion, (from Canaan,) is unsettled. The fact remains as witnessed by Rawlinson, Sharpe, and others, that the intellectual type was engrafted upon the Indo-Hamitic, and not at an earlier date than 2500 B. C., (our plan of chronology). The grandeur of this new epoch, in its peculiar line of development, can never be expressed in human language. Its nearest approach is in the mighty monuments whose lofty summits and outline majesty still defy the hand of Time.

We may hope for accuracy in one statement:—That Lower Egypt, (Memphite,) was peopled by Mizraimites—an Hamitic branch, of Mongolian type, as represented in the facial and cranial type of Fig 24.

Syncellus tells us that Egypt was governed by a threefold race of kings. The first were the Mestræi (Mezrites, Mitzraimites), as noted. 2d, The Auritæ, a "foreign dynasty of shepherd kings," who, according to Josephus, were dominant in Egypt for five centuries—an epoch which closes at 1879 B.C. Manetho recognizes these Auritæ, though he gives to them a different number and duration. The third race of kings were native Egyptians.

Analyze the early history of Egypt and see when these Auritæ must have appeared. Very few will differ from us in stating that the first conquest of Thebes was Memphite, under Cheops. Who was this Cheops of whom we have spoken?

Cheops is described as a foreigner, a man who abused the Egyptians, insulted their gods, destroyed their temples and crushed the priesthood—later in life "repented and WROTE A RELIGIOUS WORK on the gods!"

Now who were the Auritæ? "They are said to have come from the East; to have set fire to the towns, and overturned the temples"—to have been in a state of constant hostility with the natives, "and the close of their dynasty, 500 years in extent, was in 1700."

In view of the improbability of two conquests of Egypt by shepherd kings during this period, it may be stated, with deference, that Cheops was the first of the Auritæ, and that during the 500 years of their reign, they firmly planted their race type upon the soil of the Nile valley. The erasure of the shepherd cartouches from the monuments of this era—the consequent ignorance of them by the Egyptians; their want of knowledge regarding that one Great Pyramid—all add to the value of this opinion.

It may also be stated that at this early day an important modification of the Egyptian hieroglyphics may be traced. The early Aryan and Semitic types of picture writing were distinguished by a predominance of the vowel elements; the Coptic by nearly an absence of vowels and preponderance of the consonants. But at some time during this thousand years vowels appear in such quantity as to indicate a new element in stone literature. Also the correlation between the age-characters and personal attributes of the Cheops of Heroditus and the Suphis of Manetho—the fourth Memphian and the sixth Egyptian dynasties—points unmistakably in the direction that all these finger marks of that period do—viz.: that at or just before the Memphian conquest of Thebes all Egypt was invaded by a more intellectual race of people; that they left their marks on the monumental history and the facial and cranial angles; and on the national character of the hitherto Hindoo—and Hamitic, occupants of the valley. Their life channel may be traced in its one grand tradition—its origin from Menes. Its Menes came from Menu of India, and it went, 1000 years later, into Attic theotechny as Minos. There is also one channel in which a search among the traditions of the invading race is confined; and that is in the stream of theosophy older than Menu, Sabeism, or the perpetual fires of Iran—the monotheism of the race *kindred* to the Abrahamic, of whom Melchi-Zedek is the earliest pontiff-king! If the philosophy of this singular history teaches us of this invasion of the shepherd kings at this time, it teaches that they were subsequently expelled, though not conquered. Still another dim circumstance adds to the mystery of this invasion. During this period some "sacred books" were "written." Not stone books but *papyrus* books—and yet the "sacred writing" was the stone hieroglyphic system! The books are lost, of course. A whole race of kings let them alone, to crumble, and so did the priesthood. How could this have been if they were about the worship of the Sun-God, or Apis the god of life? At last a king searched his kingdom for them—and though he was unsuccessful in finding them, fragments of this same work have probably been secured,* —and they read much like monotheistic doctrine. A few sentiments are given from M. Chabas' translation:

"If it may be humbling to thee to serve a wise man,

These fragments were found in the tombs of the "Acthoes" during "2d Thinite, 5th Elephantine, 6th Memphian, ninth Heracleopolite, 11th Diospolite," (Theban), dynasties. It seems the Acthœ king, in the eyes of Egyptian priests was "wicked," that he was eaten up by alligators—after going mad; and all his Acthoite successors, with one exception, were called Nantef—so wicked were they. Their tombs are found near ancient Heracleopolis. Could the "writings" of such a race of kings be in accord thy conduct will be be good with GOD, for he knows that thou art among the little ones. Do not make thy heart proud against him."

"Obedience is loved by God. [Obedience to what?] Disobedience is hated by him. To hear the WORD,† to love, to obey, *that* is to fulfill good precept."

"What the wise know to be death, that is his life every day."

The importance of a close review of this age, will appear under the head of History of the Pyramid.

EGYPTIAN SCIENCE.

Before closing the chapter, we feel compelled to refer to one or two points of general interest, as describing this epoch.

In astronomy, the Egyptians were exceedingly backward, and in meteorology, and season divisions, their system was such as to convince the most skeptical, that no true system of cosmology, could originate among them.

The year was divided into three seasons: The season of Vegetation, (Fig 26) embraces four months; the season of Harvest, four months,(27), and season of Inundation four months. (28). This was in the pyramid epoch. Every month was divided into thirty days, (Fig. 26.), giving 360 days to the year. This made the year five days short and the consequence can be readily surmised. "New years" steadily receded, until the period of vegetation may have been in the middle of the inundation season, or during the dry and sandy harvest! "At some unknown time" says

---

with Egyptian polytheism? It may be proper to state that the Heracleopolite king who was not called "Nantef" was exceedingly popular and powerful in Egypt, and seemed to live in harmony with Coptic theology.

*This cannot refer to the innumerable deities of the Egyptians, nor to Ra, nor the translated Menes. The very signification of the term, and the doctrine implied, are foreign to Siriad theosophy.

†Does not sound hieratic or polytheistic.

one writer, "five days were added," to correct the cycle, this probably did not occur until some Greek philosopher, or Phœnician conqueror, subsequent to B.C. 1200, brought them to a realizing sense of the year's true length and corrected a most remarkable peripatesis.

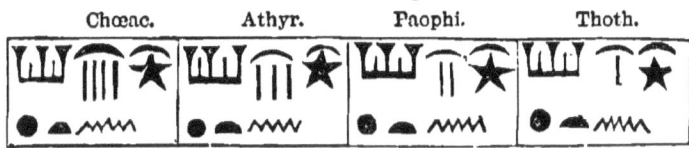

Fig. 26. Season of Vegetation.

Not until Eratosthenes, (270 B.C.), did the Egyptians know anything, so to speak, regarding the true science of astronomy. It was then demonstated by this mathematician, an ornament of the Greek School of Alexandria,

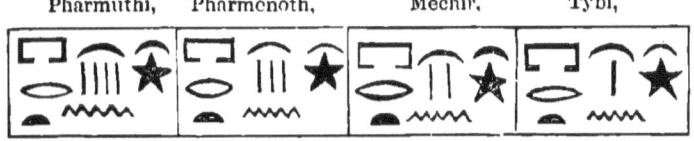

Fig. 27. Season of Harvest.

and keeper of Ptolemy Euergetes' library, that the earth was a ball. He also discovered a method of fixing lati-

Fig. 28. Season of Inundation.

tudes, by observing the shadows, at noon, at different places on equinoctial days. (Fig. 29). He also calculated the circumference of the earth by this method. (Fig. 30). He ascertained the obliquity of the ecliptic, by measuring the sun's shadow at the same place on the longest and shortest days of the year. He placed the circumference of the earth at 250,000 *Stadia*.

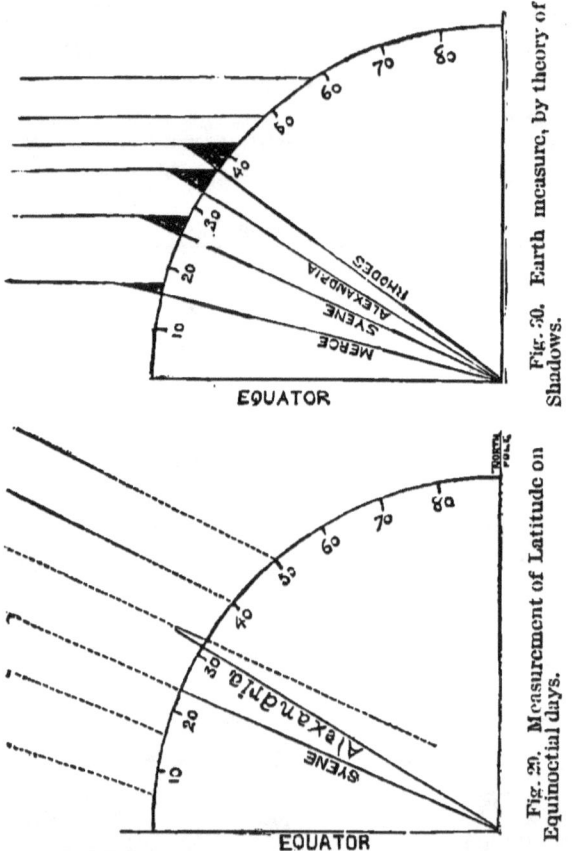

Fig. 30. Earth measure, by theory of Shadows.

Fig. 29. Measurement of Latitude on Equinoctial days.

Still neither Eratosthenes the Greek, nor Manetho the Egyptian, undertook to translate the hieroglyphs for future generations.

There is a widespread belief among many people, even students, that the ancient Egyptians were a highly developed race, intellectually. Yet it is an error as far as it refers to the pre-Ptolemaic period. In astronomy, mathematics, chemistry, art, economics, (witness the processes of irrigation), literature, painting, sculpture, (æsthetic), perspective, etc., they were singularly and persistently backward. In the midst of the grand mausoleums, and monuments of ancient Egypt, down to five or six hundred years before Christ, no *arch* relieves the severe angular

Fig. 31.   Month.   Half-month.   Week. (U-K).

structures. In astronomy, the sun moved around from east to west in its risings. Its figures came from Arabia. Its letters changed not from sound-pictures. Its tomb paintings were daubs. Yet in massiveness, in grandeur, in lofty and enduring structure, it overreached its own history. During the comparatively modern Alexandrian epoch, however, it became the seat of Grecian culture. The obelisk ceased, and literature developed—not Egyptian, but Grecian.

Fig. 32. Names of Egypt in Hieroglyphs.

FRAGMENTS.

The thirty dynasties of Egyptian sovereigns are by some placed continuously, one following the other. The more advanced idea, however, is that many of them are contemporaneous. It would be contrary to the philosophy of general history that the Thinite, Theban, Memphite, Heracleopolite, Elephantine, and other independent kingdoms should co-exist more or less, in different ages, while their monarchs were distinct and successive. The following table represents the opinions of several authorities:

No. of Dynasty.	LeSuer. Marietta Bey, Renan. B.C.	Lepsius, Bunsen, Fergusson. B.C.	Lane, Gardner Wilkin'n Rawl'sn. B.C.	Osborn's astron'cl Calculations. B.C.	By our Analysis B.C.
1	5735	3892	2700	2429	2800
2	5472	3639	2480	2430	
3	5170	3338	2670	2329	
4	4996	3124	2440	2228	2200
5	4472	2840	2440	2228	
6		2744	2200	2107	1000
7		2592	1800		
8		2522	1800		
9		2674	2200	2107	
10		2565		1959	
11		2423	2200	2107	
12	3435	2380	2080		
13		2136	1920		
14		2167	2080		
15		2101	2080	1900	
16		1842	1800	1900	1700

We do not think the above table wholly just to Wilkinson. In the "Topography of Thebes" he puts Menes at 2201, and Suphis at 2123, about the same date as we have adopted for the latter.

One of the most remarkable misconceptions of the duty of the historian occurs in the work of Wilkinson referred to. On page 506 he says: "I am aware that the era of Menes might be carried to a much more remote period than the date I have assigned it; but as we have as yet no authority further than the uncertain statements of Manetho's copyists, to fix the time and number of the reigns intervening between his accession and that of Apappus, [Apoph. Maximus. Time of Abraham's visit. 1900.], I have not placed him earlier FOR FEAR of interfering with the date of the deluge of Noah, WHICH IS 2348 B. C." This is heroic confidence in Dr. Usher, though hard on the Septuaginta, by whom the Flood was placed a great many centuries before 2348 B. C. The Samaritans, perhaps, who do likewise, also deserve some consideration.

Before any definite era in Egyptian history, the territory lying between the Red Sea and Assyria, including Shinar, Sodom, Gomorrah, Edom, (Petrea), Ellasur, Goim; Salem, capital of what was afterwards Judea, with Melchi-Zedek for priest and king; Gomar, ruled by Abi-melech; the cities of Philisto-Arabia, and tribes of nomads, were all more or less familiar with the doctrine of monotheism—of one God, "one, ineffable, invisible, all-powerful," as taught in La-outse's "Four Kings."

A comprehensive view of the Indo-Syrio-Coptic races, their locations, traditions and migrations, leads us to believe that an invasion of Egypt

EARLY HISTORY OF EGYPT.

before the Hellenic era would result in the erection of monotheistic monuments.

Zincke, Vicar to the Queen, in 1871, gave the Nile markings of annual overflow on the granite hills at Semneh more chronological credit than they deserve. He states that "in every instance [of these inscriptions] the date is given." As he gives this particular record great importance in making the early Egyptian epochs extremely ancient, he should distinguish between the numbered cartouche of a king, and a chronological date. There were no cycles, or other methods of astronomical chronology, established in the times of Osirtesen and Amenemha.

Baldwin, in "Pre-Historic Nations," rests much of his excessive antiquity of Egypt on evidence like the following: "You Greeks are novices in antiquity. The history of 8000 years is deposited in our sacred books, but I can ascend to a much higher antiquity, and tell you what our fathers have done for 9000 years." This was said to Solon by an Egyptian priest several centuries B. C. Not a fragment of Solon's writings, if there ever were any, remains. Plato and others, who had gathered up some of his teachings, preserve his memory. But the value of the evidence is not only lessened by its age, oral character, garbling, and the known tendencies of the Egyptian priests: It is well known that the supreme effort of the priesthood of that age was to establish the certainty and renown of the Gods, especially the deified mortals who reigned on earth. This only could be accomplished through the mysticism of antiquity. It is ludicrous, frequently, to see them leap from some well-known personage, like Darius Hystaspes, 10,000 years backward to Zoroaster, who was nearly contemporaneous with the former. Such testimony will not stand unsupported.

"Shemmo" is the Egyptian name of the foreigners known as the Shepherd race, who were driven out by Chebros-Amosis. They are thought by all historians to have been Canaanites. It will be remembered in this connection that "Chemmis" is the name given to Cheops by some ancient writers; also applied to Suphis. Amid the uncertainty, it is probable that the Cheopian race were the Shemmo of Egypt.

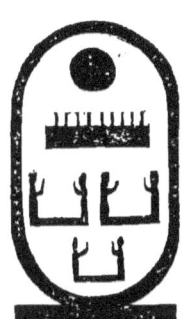
Mencophra.

According to Manetho, Queen Nitocris built the smallest of the three pyramids of Ghizeh. The name of King Mecora or Mencophra (Fig. 33) was found on the wooden sarcophagus in the underground chamber. Probably Mecora was the Theban name for the Memphite king Thothmosis III, (Fig. 21), to whom the third pyramid is credited.

"Spherical Trigonometry appears to have been wholly unknown in Ancient Egypt."—Kenrick.

The same writer says: "The fact that the pyramids are placed with their sides exactly facing the cardinal points, shows that in the early age when these structures were erected, they had the means of tracing an accurate meridian line. To accomplish this requires rather time and care than great astronomical knowledge. It is effected by the observation of the shadow of a gnomon, at the time of the solstices."

Mr. Kenrick is doubtless correct in the first statement. It is natural, therefore, to expect from him an hypothesis as to how the trigonometrical relations of the Great Pyramid were established! It was built, and built in sublime proportions, and far more correctly than modern structures of monumental character. The second statement is peculiar for so eminent an authority. The practical knowledge either of a gnomon or the solstices was wanting in a race that figured 11,340 years from Menes to Sethos, (Herodtius), during which time the sun moved around the earth, in its rising, sideways, four times! Hipparchus lived 15 centuries after the pyramid epoch.

A GREAT MYSTERY.

Fig. 34. View of the Pyramids during the inundation season, from the Nile.

HISTORY OF THE PYRAMID.

TWO great cities controlled the Nile Valley during the earlier history—Thebes and Memphis. The latter was situated near the fork of the Delta. Parallel with the left bank of the west fork, stretching from Alexandria in the Northwest to Dongal and Nubia in the South, and sinking away westward under the desert sands—is a range of low-browed mountains. This is the Libyan chain. Where it draws near the Nile, a few miles farther above the forks, close to where once the powerful and populous city of Memphis sent forth her armies, on the west bank, is a broad, broken plateau, known as the hill of Ghizeh. It is a barren, and unsightly waste of rock and sand, painfully reflecting the glare of midday suns and glamour of unclouded moons. No spot on earth could have been selected more intensely disagreeable for human habitation or human glory—excepting the interior desert, on the confines of which we find the hill of Gizeh.

Yet here is the acme of all human efforts for fame. In the very darkest hour before the dawn of civilization, human hands reared upon this spot the most extensive and enduring monuments our planet has ever seen. Here has science spanned 4000 years of time. Genius gazes with awe, and Skill shouts with admiration. Here, too, Napoleon fought a most remarkable battle—demonstrating the wonder in military science of a hollow square—a battle which, says Alexander Dumas, decided the conflict between the East and the West. Here are the Pyramids.

There are some sixty pyramidal structures remaining in Egypt—and the half-obliterated ruins of many more. But the three which crown the hill of Ghizeh are objects of more especial study; and of these three the greatest, the Pyramid of Ghizeh, is the first and foremost wonder of the world.

On the west bank of the Nile, between the hill and the river, is the village of Ghizeh. On the east bank are the battered relics of "Old Cairo," now sometimes known as Fostat or Babylon, and a few miles farther to the north and east is Cairo, the capital of modern Egypt. From Cairo to the Pyramids is usually a distance of ten miles, but during the inundation it is fully twenty, by the necessarily circuitous route. One expression is in the mouth of every traveller who visits the Pyramid from Cairo:—"We thought them near by, and much overrated in magnitude. But wearily passing mile after mile, we found that their incomparable size deceived us—the distance was great and their proportions beyond description!"

The Pyramid of Ghizeh stands upon a shelf of rock 150 feet above the desert, and from 130 to 140 above the Nile. It is not alone either in its majesty or historic significance. Besides the two other large pyramids, there is another monument, of rude art but grand proportions, which is at least twenty-four centuries old. It is the Sphynx. There are also innumerable tombs, above and below the surface, in every degree of preservation, or rather destruction.

Without entering into discussion, we can justly observe

HISTORY OF THE PYRAMID. 53

that there is no evidence that leads us to believe any Siriad monument now standing, is older than the Great Pyramid. The expression of such an opinion is often met, but the evidences are such that no reliance can be placed upon them. If the remains of such a pyramid present a broader base, than that at Ghizeh, and is shorn of its height, it is at once observed that *time* has worn it down. Time does not do such exact execution as to clear off the

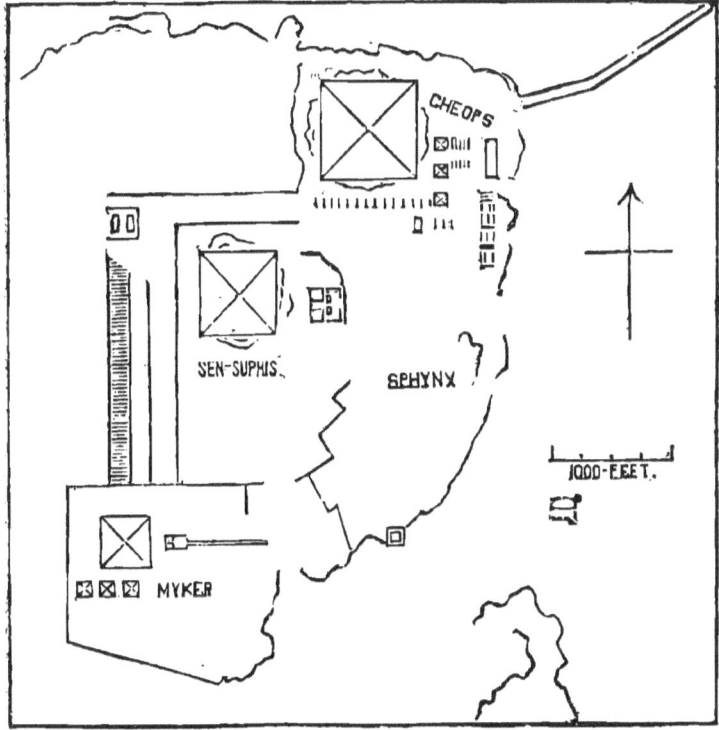

Fig. 25. Plan of the location of the monuments on the Hill of Ghizeh. Remains of the great causeway in upper right hand corner.

vast superstructure, leaving a few level tiers much less worn! Nor have the modern monarchs used the material for building, when more recent cities are nearer other monuments and quarries. Probably such ruins are the remains of uncompleted pyramids. Neither is it good judgment to give ruins of brick structures, however vast, a date antecedent to the blast-worn and earthquake-rent, rock-built memorials which have outlasted them! Turning to the *history* of monumental Egypt, but this one Pyramid is heard from in the Ancient day—one which suddenly springs into the world's architecture, as a parent of the multitude of imitations which follow it. Never has there been a day in recorded time when *The* Pyramid was not looking out upon the world in solemn majesty.

Arabian writers say it was built before the deluge. A very wonderful thought that! Its shape, its substance, possibly its *mission*, may have preserved it from the wrath of the elements, to give to the survivors that cosmogony which an antecedent population possessed. Unfortunately for this hypothesis there are abundant evidences of a later period. The causeway, the *debris*, (chips), the hieroglyphs in the hidden masonry, and the older histories, all give substantial clues to its epoch.

Perizonius, and quite a number of mediæval writers, ascribe it to the Israelites. Dr. Clarke also shoulders it upon the Israelites, as the tomb of Joseph; who, however, was disgraced by a Pharaoh who "knew not Joseph" nor respected his descendants. Heroditus calculates their erection at two or three hundred years before Cambyses, (or about seven or eight hundred years B.C.). Conder concludes that 1000 years B.C. was not too modern a date.

Although Heroditus has informed us that the date was only about twelve generations before Cambyses, he ascribes its erection to Cheops and his brother, which would date at least 2000 years B.C. Eratosthenes refers it to Suphis, of Manetho. Diodorus merely repeats the opinions of other writers, speaking of Chemmis, (Cheops), Cephren and Mycerinus first. Pliny is silent. Josephus ascribes it to the Hebrews. Manetho, the Egyptian Priest, gives Suphis as the builder, who is usually regarded as the same as Cheops, Chemmis, Saophis, or Chofo. His cartouche, or hierogiyphic oval, was found on the masonry in Davidson's chamber, as also his brothers. (Cephren.)

There is an ancient tradition, quoted by several writers, (referred to in Chapter on Early History,) of a shepherd people of India, the Pali, who once conquered Egypt, and the Pyramid has been ascribed to them. The Yoingees have also been referred to. Mr. Gliddon, the eminent American Egyptologist, states that the direct descendants of Ham, the Mizraimites, were the builders. Aristotle declared that they were built by despots to keep the people poor. Josephus relates a tradition of the descendants of Noah, (Shemites), erecting two monuments, one of brick and one of stone, in Egypt, on which (or "in" which) they represented astronomical science. This is an exceedingly important tradition. It deserves more consideration than any tradition which has been called to our attention, although no Pyramidical writer has properly elaborated its value.

In the first place, this ascription of the structure to the direct descendants of Noah, does not conflict with the direct and conside.able testimony from Hindoo sources, including the Pali and the Yoinge narrations, which are Semitic in origin. Nor does it interfere with the opinion that the Caphtorim built it, (Canaanites, supposed to have been the Hyksos). Nor does it shut out the Biblical pre-Abrahamic race under the High-Priesthood of Melchizedec. Secondly, it comes from a source more valuable than all other testimonies, (the Egyptian monuments being silent.)—viz: the Jewish race. This race kept a record by ancestral history, by tablets, and by books,—some of which are lost, which date back 1000 years before the earliest written record elsewhere extant, excepting the Siriad hieroglyphs, which may have been contemporaneous. The race was in full accord with the doctrines of monotheism, which *seem* to be developed in the Pyramid. Thirdly, while the Jewish record *may* have been contemporaneous with the race of pyramid builders, we know that the Greek and Alexandrian races, languages, and literature originated many centuries (possibly fifteen) *after* the erection. Fourthly, the Bible speaks of it, and by inferences makes it the work of such a race. Even the Sabeans state that it was built by the children of Seth.

If it were built by this race, (Shemites), then it was by the Hyksos invaders

Prof. Piazzi Smyth, Dr. Seiss, and almost all modern writers take a view of the origin of the Pyramid analogous to the following:—The cartouches in the Pyramid read "Shofo" or Shopho, and Kephren (Cephren). Shopho was the Cheops of Heroditus, and Suphis of Manetho. (According to M. Chabas these are the natural renditions of Koufou). A very great many evidences now known point strongly to this personage as the builder. Heroditus states, of Cheops and his brother Kephren: "No Egyptian will mention their names; but they always attribute *their* Pyramids to one Philit on, (Philitis), a shepherd, who kept his cattle in those parts." Subsequently both these foreigners [*what* foreigners we are not told' unless it were the Cheopians, as inferred in our Early History,—possibly the "S latian foreigners" of the previous chapter], were induced to leave Egypt with 240,000 men, and they went into Canaan and built Jerusalem—or "Salem." The conclusion is that a certain Philitis with his tribe of Semites were a monotheistic race of Philistines, who overcame Cheops, ["without a battle"], and built the Pyramid, and that Philitis was Melchizedec.

Part of this conclusion seems quite possible: That foreigners built the Pyramid; that they were Canaanites or Shemites; also that Melchizedek *may* have been Philitis and their High-Priest is not impossible—it may be probable. But that Philitis built the Pyramid seems a very great strain upon probabilities. Instead of the reference to the matter by Heroditus being an historical conclusion, it seems rather a very satirical effort to rob Cheops, a terrible god-destroyer, of his credit, by referring the great life work to his "goat-herd." Heroditus must have looked at it thus, by the use of the word we have italicised—"*their*,"—"their pyramids"—and not "his" (Philitis). The logical deduction from the construction is, that Heroditus regarded the matter as an effort to belittle both Cheops and his pyramid. Nor is it quite reasonable to believe that Philitis was Melchi-zedek, if the latter were the builder of Jerusalem. For that 240,000 went out of Egypt, probably, during the reign of Chebros-Amosis, several generations afterward.

Lord Lindsay says the royal shepherds of Egypt probably built them, afterwards becoming the Philistines. We can only remark that the entire history of the Egyptians teaches us that the people were not shepherds in any sense —having few, or no pastures, and hating both the *wool* for clothing and the flesh for food. Sharpe does not believe that Philistine Hyksos built the Pyramid, but his remark is based on the evidence of the word Philitis alone.

One thing is certain—that impenetrable darkness surrounds the history of the Pyramid's construction. We come to one conclusion, amid many conjectures:—that it was built by Cheops, a foreigner, and by a foreign race —the Hyksos.

The Pyramid, as a whole, was a work of such immense magnitude that no nation of to-day could furnish the labor, treasure, or material, for continuous construction. But in detail it is not composed of such immense blocks of stone as many infer, nor does it demand such an excess of engineering skill that modern science can not repeat it. It was said by Heroditus that it required the labor of 100,000 men for twenty years. This is a reasonable statement, for labor in Egypt was, and still is, given by the population for bare subsistence. The only requirement was that Cheops should feed his hundred thousand, and scantily cloth them. Scarcely a nation in Europe is doing less than this to-day—not to mention the vast and costly armaments that accompany them. But while nations can get soldiers now for a pittance, *per capita*, they cannot get artisans so cheaply as did Cheops. It is supposed that much of the stone was floated down the Nile, and brought a great distance—a matter of no great wonder, in view of the more remarkable quarries of Baalbec, and other ruined capitals. Remains of the immense causeways between the pyramids and the Nile, still remain, (Fig. 35). Vast collections of debris, or stone chips, also exist in the neighborhood.

There are many methods given as the probable manner of raising the stones up the giddy terrace, and subsequently coating with finer marble. Few of these are worthy of serious attention, and as they are wholly supposititious it will not be discussed here. However, the plan of construction is worthy of attention as it has been the subject of much study and especially by Mr. Glidden. The illustration, from "*Egyptian Archæology*," (Fig. 36), represents his views. "A" represents a vertical section of a pyramid, the foundations of which rest on the rock at an elevation above the level of cultivation. At "D" is a chamber hollowed out for sepulture. Over it is reared, by following generations, a succession of layers of masonry, until a certain size is attained, when smaller stone, or even rubble, ("B"), complete it. Over this is added, still in terra-

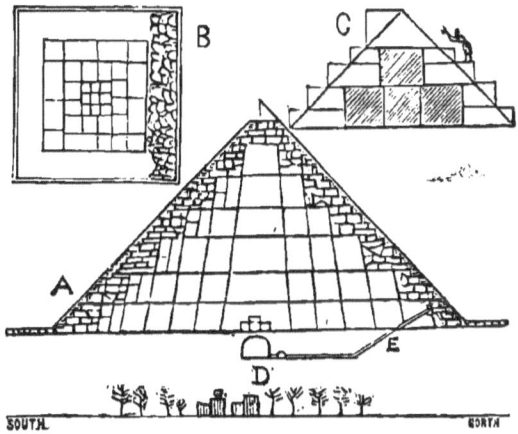

Fig. 36. Sectional view of pyramids representing Glidden's views of construction.

ces, blocks of finer quality. Then the laborers begin at the summit and chip downward, as at "C," leaving a symmetrical pile. There seem many unreasonable features in this hypothesis. After generations do not usually labor so extensively for dead relatives, as to absorb a nation's purse and power. Osborn wholly rejects the plan. The probability is that in the case of other pyramids, which were tombs, the dumb sleepers within reared them for the perpetuity of their own memory. Alas! the stones remain but the names are fled! It is not at all certain that the Great Pyramid, the first and grandest, ever contained a corpse.

With this diversion regarding its character, let us return to its history. Being moderately certain that it was built during the first 1000 years of Egyptian history, and by Cheops, or Suphis, we put its date between 2500 and 2000 B.C., 1900 being the time of Abraham's visit. The former (2500) is the proximate date given by Wilkinson, Rawlinson and Lane, and 2228 is given by Osborn.

Sharpe, however, comes down to 1700, and a few Egyptologists struggle with 5700 B.C. There have been writers who scored the date 1000 B.C.

With the exception of the Bible, Heroditus' writings furnish the earliest reference to it. This historian visited Egypt about 445 B.C., and described to some extent both the Pyramid and its causeway for transportation of materials. The priests who gave Heroditus information regarding it, stated that it was the tomb of Cheops, who was buried far beneath it, on a rock surrounded by water, admitted from the Nile by a secret passage. This was undoubtedly an ignorant superstition, as there are no passages leading any distance below the subterranean chamber, and the level of the Nile is 164 feet beneath the base of the Pyramid at low water. It was also stated that at least the causeway was covered with inscriptions, and one was represented as having ornamented the Pyramid. Of this Heroditus says:—

"There was signified on the Pyramid, by means of Egyptian characters, how much was expended on radishes, onions, and garlic for the laborers; and as I well remember, the interpreter, reading over the characters to me, said, that it amounted to one thousand and six hundred talents of silver."

We are happy to state that Heroditus ridiculed this

rendition of the inscription, stating that even the rock-inscribing of the cost of iron tools, bread and clothing would b· more important. There is at present no such silly hieroglyphs present on the monuments.

The tendency of Egyptian rock-history is to develop greatness, or lofty attributes, powers and merit, and not the supposed-to-be-eternal literature of the simplest food of a race of slaves whom Cheops would have whistled to his side as he would a dog!

A pioneer in pyramid science, Mr. John Taylor, first quoting from Dr. Thomas Young regarding the nature of hieratic writing, declares that the figures in stone of radishes, onions and garlic, were characters representing certain important pyramid relations. For instance, he supposes the radishes to have represented degrees (°) of longitude, or latitude, the onions, minutes, (') and the double root of the garlic seconds (''). Nor is this theory untenable when the facts of its interior symbolisms are examined.

This inscription is of great importance, nor should we lightly pass it by. It is not unreasonable to suppose the interpreter for Heroditus was an ignoramus, even though a priest—and there is little evidence as to his caste.

Heroditus wrote about 445 B.C. We know that the knowledge of hieroglyphs had gradually faded from Egyptian education—that two centuries after Heroditus, a Sybennite priest of unusual acquirements prepared a key by which to translate them. The Grecian mind, with its alphabet and philosophy, was driving out the *intellect* of the servile race.* Hence, it is not probable that a guide

---

*Ibin Abd Alkokem, an Arabian philosopher, stated that among the learned men of Egypt he could find no certain information regarding the Pyramid.

who led Heroditus around, possibly as a hired servant, could read the mystical lore. Again, knowing that Egyptian priests, from time immemorial, hated Cheops, his memory and his monuments, how natural for one who would refer its construction to a goat-herd to be-little the sublimest record the sun ever lighted, before his Grecian pay-master! How much to be regretted that the inscription was not pictorially presented—the most ancient sentence bequeathed to the human race! While the Egyptians as a race were ignorant of circle mensuration, we have reason to "know" that the builder of the Pyramid was familiar with almost every now-known principle in geometry in its ancient as well as modern application, and plane and spherical trigonometry. There is a statement in old Coptite books to this effect: On the pyramids was an inscription which said, "I, Saurid, the king, built the Pyramids in such and such a time, and finished them in six years; he that comes after me and says that he is equal to me, let him destroy them in six hundred years; and yet it is known that it is easier to pluck down than to build; and when I finished them, I covered them with Sattin and let him cover them with slats."—(Greaves). If this Arabian translation of a Coptic tradition were not akin to the "Arabian Nights" in origin and date, it would be of value. We deferentially suggest to Mr. Bonwick the idea that his recent work on the Pyramids would be more valuable, if he remembered and mentioned the comparative value of many such excerpts.

In giving the Bible references to the Pyramid, we plunge into disputed territory, but the general discussion of this belongs to another chapter.

Portions of the Bible were doubtless written as early as

1600 B. C., and the Edomitic work (Job) may have been contemporaneous with the later years of the first Hyksos.

The spirit of the Abrahamic fatherhood over his descendants makes even a statement as late as Jeremiah, (750 B. C.), of far more value than the chance light thrown by a solitary historian of early Greece; and inasmuch as the claim is distinctly set forth that the God of Israel built, or directed the building of the Pyramid, it is best to analyze its allusions well. But much of this will come under the head of the sixth statement of the "Analysis." There is much evidence that the Israelites were familiar with the Pyramid, and, though strange as it may appear, were in the habit of ascribing its erection to divine impulse. Although, as a matter of history, there is no word connecting the Pyramid with the Hebrews, as represented elsewhere, it was undoubtedly erected by a Semitic race whose origin was either in direct line with Abraham, or related to him through Shem and Noah.

And this race of Shemites or Semites were the peculiar inheritors and propagators of the religious wisdom which the world has accepted in the Bible, and is not unlikely to accept in the Pyramid—the one through Abraham, the other through Melchizedek. There has been an impression abroad that the Hebrews themselves, either under Joseph's ministry, or while in servitude, erected this vast structure. But this was quite impossible; nor, when we view the whole history of the valley, filled with works of magnitude and grandeur, does it seem that its erection— as far as the manual labor was concerned—was beyond the possibilities of Egypt during any ancient epoch. The Israelites were not in Egypt before 1750 B. C. Abraham lived 1900 B. C. The Pyramid was doubtless built 21 or 2200, B. C. Its own date is 2170, B. C. Again, the Bible speaks of the labor of the Hebrews as consisting of brick work, a more modern architecture than the stone era.

Had the Great Pyramid of Egypt been a part of the Abrahamic "Logos," it would have been referred to in the Bible as the direct mission of the Israelites in Egypt.

On the other hand, the Bible references are just such as would occur if the Pyramid were a mystic testimony to them, of the same God, by a kindred and antecedent race—the real mysteries of which were one day to be disclosed.*

The most remarkable item in the history of the Pyramid is that its interior passages were immediately closed after completion. Not only was it closed on the surface, but that ascending passage was so completely blocked by an immense stone portcullis that to this day it has never been removed. If the Pyramid were built in the year 2170 B. C., then during the growth and ascendency of the Assyrian Empire; the development of the Abrahamic succession to Shem; the genesis of the Hebrew nation through the children of Israel; the singular existence of Edom; the rise and commercial eminence of Syrio-Phœnician Tyre; the evolution of Hellenic nationality; the founding of Rome; the decadence of Greece; the triumphs and decline of the eternal city; the destruction of Jerusalem; the Birth and crucifixion of Christ; the vast aggregation of papal power, and the Hegira of Mahomet; the lapse into the "dark ages;"—during all these bubbling, seething, changing years of humanity's history, those cavernous records of sublime intelligence were closed. Why?

The limestone facing of the Great Pyramid was removed

---

*This proposition will be peculiarly acceptable to those who have studied the recently startling discoveries regarding "Anglo-Israelitism." Any person who desires to study the Pyramid should investigate this subject —for it is rapidly assuming importance in the ethnology of Europe.

long before any modern writer described it. Still, the entrance by which we now pass in was unknown until opened by interior excavations.*

In the year 825 A. D., Caliph Al Mamoun, the Mahommedan ruler of Cairo, became convinced that vast treasure was stored within the Pyramid. He set men at work with fire, chisels, and vinegar, to open the heart of the mystery. Months of anxious expectation and deferred hope made the hearts of his laborers sick, for the dark, hot, dusty hole they projected was slowly piercing the very heart of the mountain, but no treasure nor mystery

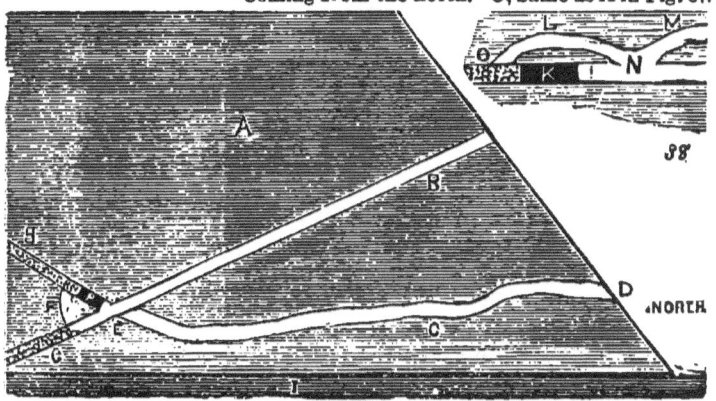

Fig. 38. Horizontal section of passage around portcullus, K. N, Junction of Al Mamoun's hole and original passage. M, Coming from the north. O, Same as H in Fig. 37.

Fig. 37. D, C, E, F, Passage cut by Al Mamoun's laborers. A, Masonry. B, Original entrance, closed and forgotten in Al Mamoun's time. F, Passage cut around the portcullus, same as L in F g. 38. G, Descending passage closed with rubbish. H, Ascending passage, filled with loose rocks. P, Portcullus.

was unveiled. Mutterings and discontent informed the Caliph that to go much farther with such onerous labor and such draughts on his treasury would threaten revolution. One hundred feet were passed and still solid rock

*The Romans are said to have discovered the entrance by removal of a stone over the opening.

before them. In the thick and heavy air the workmen dropped their primitive tools and gave up the task. A few moments more and the great effort to pierce the Pyramid would have been over, and the world have henceforth regarded the ancient pile, as Al Mamoun would have done—a solid pyramid of masonry! What other person would have subjected himself, after such a trial, to the laugh of the world, and the great waste of means, to do the same thing over? There was a "destiny" as some would say—a "Providence," as most will insist, in what occurred. In the midst of such silence that the heart's beating could be heard,* while nerveless Arabs were gleaming upon each other with suspicious eyes and rebellious hearts, and the dim torches casting sepulchral shadows in the narrow way—a dull, heavy sound, as of falling masonry, was heard near them, but farther within the rock. Every man sprang to his work, and in the direction of the sound they soon burst into a passageway of most wonderful finish and polish! Now indeed were the treasures of Araby's day dream within reach! A few steps into the darkness, and lo! The passage (open alone in the ascending direction) was blocked by an immense portcullus of stone, which defied all human efforts to remove. The passage downwards was disguised by a mass of stone and rubbish thrown down in previous ages.

And what was most interesting, this upward passage would not have been known but for the *falling of the stone.*

These now hopeful Arabs soon dug around the massive block, (Fig. 37), and found the passage above filled with rubble stone and broken rock. It was a laborious task to remove these one by one; but when accomplished, says

---
*As in Mammoth cave.

HISTORY OF THE PYRAMID.

Dr. Seiss.—"Up and up the smooth and long ascending floor-lines the marauders pushed their slippery and doubtful way, till near the end of the Grand Gallery. Then they clambered over a three-foot step, then bowed their heads beneath a low door-way, bounded on all sides with awful blocks of frowning red granite; and then leaped without further hindrance, into the Grand Chamber, the first to enter since the Great Pyramid was built."

But the crest'fallen Ishmaelites found nothing but an empty stone chest, known as the coffer or sarcophagus.

The failure to find treasure, it is said, so enraged the laborers that Al Mamoun pretended to find enough gold to pay all the expenses, buried in one of the chambers.

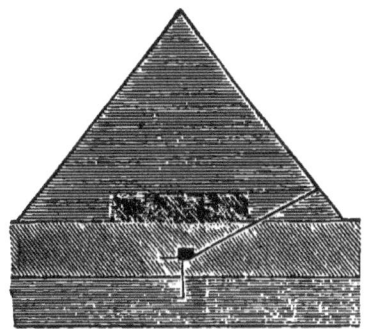
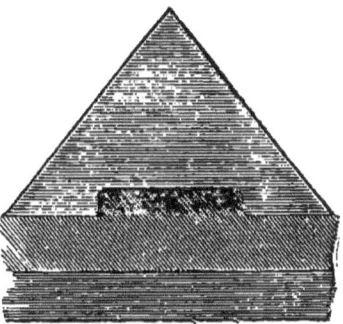

Fig. 39. The Great Pyramid 1900 years B.C.
Fig. 40. Same 600 A. D.

After this attempt, the Pyramid had a long rest. The passage of Al Mamoun became filled with rubbish, and finally obscured; the regular entrance had not been opened, and once more the dawn and nightfall of ages passed over its eternal secrets.

But the Arabs had discovered much, and it was not wholly forgotten. In the 17th and 18th centuries a general interest again became manifest among European scientists, in the Great Pyramid. Mr. Davison, who was British Consul at Algiers in 1763 spent 18 months investigating its interior, appropriating great labor and expenditure to unravel its mysteries. He also discovered the chamber of construction named after him.

But to Prof. Greaves, (1637), an enthusiastic Englishman, belongs the earlier credit of devoting toil and fortune to "Pyramidographia," the title of a work published by him. He made the first distinct attempt to get correct measurements. M. Maillet made great exertions

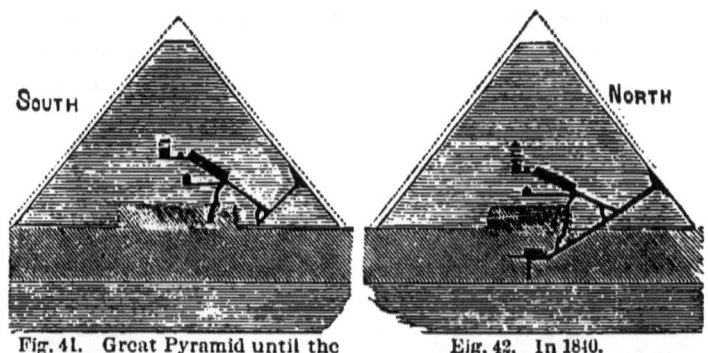

Fig. 41. Great Pyramid until the close of the eighteenth century.   Fig. 42. In 1840.

to elaborate its interior—successfully explored many passages, and altogether entered the structure for mensuration over forty times.

In 1817 Mr. Caviglia repeated the investigations of Messrs. Wood and Davison. He opened the subterranean chamber, with great trouble and danger. The French scientists under Napoleon, 1799, made extensive researches, and rendered much valuable information.

To Gen. Howard Vyse belongs great credit. He devoted his life and fortune to the development of many of the facts now so well known; reopened Al Mamoun's hole; made new excavations, and cleared out passages; found the first casing stones in the rubbish; found the four upper chambers of construction, with the hieroglyphs of Cheops or Suphis; gave remarkably correct measurements, and also opened up the neighboring pyramids.

Before us lies a volume written by a Pyramid scholar and enthusiast—John Taylor, of Leonard Place, Kensington. It was written in 1859, and the title is "The Great Pyramid. Why was it Built? And who Built i ?" He made an honest attempt to "recover *a lost leaf in the world's history.*" (The italics are his). He opened to the world the great volume of stone in the light of an Inspired Work; and in illustration brought out its mathematical, astronomical and metrical properties in strong light.

From that day to this, twenty years, his views have been developing and enlarging until many thousands of thoughtful students are in uni-on with them. He has recently passed away, but not until he saw the flame he lit radiating from Egypt over the whole world.

Prof. Piazzi Smyth, Scotland's Astronomer-Royal, took up the question in 1864, before the Royal Society, and subsequently published his work "Our Inheritance in the Great Pyramid." In a few months he determined to investigate, personally, the mighty problem. So in 1865 he visited the Pyramid, at great personal expense, with *family*, instruments, skill, knowledge, and an intense faith, to back him. His researches and measurements will be a monument to his memory. They are recorded in two works: "Life and Work at the Great Pyramid," and "Antiquity of Intellectual Man."

There have b en multitudes of other writers on this subject. Their names will appear hereafter. Let us now enter upon the direct study of the monument whose vastness and problematical character have loomed up through the ages to belittle the modern man and modern science.

The great question involved in the history of the Pyramid is—was it built as a tomb? At the time of its erection the Egyptians were in the habit of burying in a rock, and for the eminent dead, they built temples or tombs. Even Abraham was buried in a cave at Macphelah. Thousands of rock-tombs surround the pyramids. All the other pyramids were tombs, in the judgment of Egyptologists. Mummies have been found in the sarcophagi within the sepulchral chambers. But the other pyramids are all, doubtless, subsequent to the Great Pyramid, and supposing the latter to be a tomb, the builders took pattern after it. That they did not understand the entire import is evident from the fact that, 1st, the upper and symbolic chambers were sealed by a great stone which never has been removed, but is passed by digging around. And 2nd, that no attempt was ever made to follow in that direction, by constructing upper chambers in the others. Still, it is possible that Cheops, knowing the hostility of the Egyptians, built a subterranean tomb as usual—but arranged the upper chambers for utilitarian purposes,—and after death secured burial in the upper rather than the lower rooms—then sprung the mighty portcullus of stone. However this may be, and it is extremely doubtful, the symbolisms of the mighty monarch whose tomb it was or was not, still remain.

PARTS AND PROPORTIONS.

HE geometrical shape of a pyramid is familiar to all, and strangely isolated from books and society must he be who has never heard of the great pattern in the desert-bound valley of the Nile. The tumuli of prehistoric races are doubtless children of the same impulse in architecture.

In mensuration a pyramid is the same to a triangle that a cube is to a square, a sphere to a circle. The triangle, the square, the circle, measure surface, while their cognate shapes measure volume. All the pyramids of Egypt are not specially worthy of note, as exhibits of mathematical or æsthetic proportions. But the Great Pyramid of Egypt when unmutilated was a figure of remarkable properties.

Its height from the base rock to the original apex has been variously given. Many measurements were imperfect owing to the ragged character of the exterior. But Col. Howard Vyse, and Prof. Piazzi Smyth have both carefully measured it by angles established after several of the original casing stones were discovered. In 1797 the French *savans,* who made such thorough researches about the Pyramid, discovered at the corners, "sockets" in the base rock, or *"encastrements,"* which gave reasonably exact points from which to measure the base-sides and the angle of inclination. These sockets subsequently became filled and covered many feet by the drifting sands and accumulating debris, so that Col. Howard Vyse, who again uncovered them forty years after, found an Herculean task before him.

Although at least a hundred different measures have been given of the size of the Pyramid, there can now be little doubt of the approximate correctness of the following:—

Perpendicular height, from base to ancient apex, 5813.13 inches.* Length of a base side 9131 inches.

It therefore covers somewhat more than thirteen acres, and is the largest accumulation of masonry in existence. Its height is considerably more than the highest pinnacle of St. Peter's at Rome.

As stated before, it faces the cardinal points, and is only 5′ out of correct orientation. The inclined sides were once smooth and polished, with no break anywhere on the shining surface. Strabo speaks of a secret stone which could be removed and give entrance to the tomb within. We thus believe the Romans had entrance to the interior. Roman characters, it is said, were found in one of the passages. However that may be, this "secret" entrance was forgotten. About 1000 years after Christ, the Mohammedans began to strip off the marble casing to build palaces and bridges, and in the 18th century, even up to the time of Col. Vyse's explorations, it was not *known* that it ever was cased. Even now there are some hardy theorists, as there always are, who dispute the subject. While Col. Vyse was laying bare a side, down to

---

*"Pyramid" inches are always understood by the term in this work. The Pyramid inch is about .001 longer than our present inch. Dr. Seiss says one-half a fine hair's breadth. He must have seen some phenominally fine hair! The usual estimate of the height is 486 feet, length of each of the base sides 764 feet.

the "esplanade," he fortunately came in contact with two of these casing stones *in position*. Thus by the *encastremen's* discovered by the French, to give extreme corners, and these casing stones to give the precise angle of inclination, the measurements became reasonably exact.

The pyramid, as most are aware, is built in receding terraces, or tiers of masonry, and these casing stones were fitted into each tier, with great exactness, bevelled on the exterior surface, and joined or jointed with astonishing perfection. Several pieces have since been discovered and taken to Great Britain, but those of Col. Vyse were lost. These casing stones are important items in Pyra-

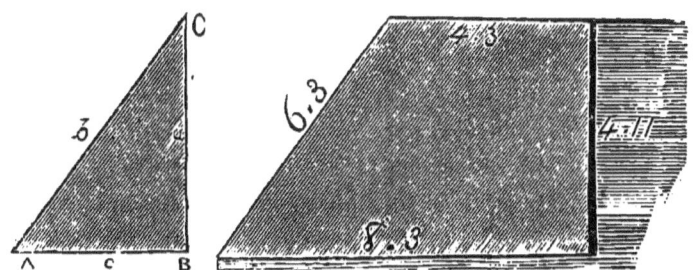

Fig. 44. and Fig. 45. Casing Stones, figures representing feet and decimals of a foot.

mid study, and we give their figure, (Fig. 45). By these casing stones the angle of inclination is ascertained, and reckoned at 51° 51′ 14.3″. But even this is taken at a mean from several calculations, as the opposite angle varies from a right angle. However, the error, if any, would be so fine that it will scarcely modify the great problems involved.

The latest deductions give the angle of inclination of the sides at 51° 49′, instead of that given above. But inasmuch as 51° 51′ 14″ is required for what is henceforth described as the *Pi* proposition, (quadrature of the circle), we retain it. Any student in engineering understands the difficulty of working in minutes, to say nothing of seconds, and how slight an error a ′ is.

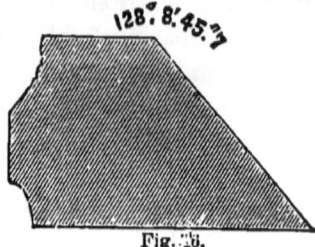
Fig. 45.

Fig. 44 represents the detached triangle by which the inclination is measured, A, B, C being not quite a right angle when drawn parallel to the edge attached to the masonry. Fig. 46 represents an elevation (sectional) of one of the casing stones, as found. The figures 128°9′45.7″ give the obtuse angle, which taken from 180° leaves 51°51′-51.4″ as the angle of inclination.

When these marble casing stones were in place, white and polished, and every joint so fine that a lens alone disclosed them; and when the unclouded sun of Araby arose over the Red Sea—reflected from its vast surface till it glowed and glinted in fiery splendor—how like a jewel from heaven must it have appeared. Picture its reflection in the changing tints of the calm and mirrored Nile!*

People who have gazed upon its shattered beauty, ignorant of the mystery within, and the ancient glory without, are still struck with a sublime appreciation—what must the *perfect Pyramid* have been?†

As the sides of the Pyramid now appear they are immense

---

*Strabo, one of the earliest Greek writers, says:—"It looked as if it had descended upon its site, ready formed from Heaven, and had not been erected by man's laborious toil." Diodorus said, "It seemed as if placed on the surrounding sand by the aid of some deity, rather than by the sole and gradual operations of man."

†"Piramona" was Coptic for "splendor of the sun." "Pi-re-nes," according to Lazerco was "splendor of the sun."

stair cases of receding tiers of masonry, each step being from two to four feet high, and in many places almost obliterated by the action of the weather, and by the visitors who send fragments of rock booming down from the summit. Still, as you look at the pile from a little distance, this terraced condition of the sides is lo.t in the grey outline. It shows how travelers differ in regard to every thing pertaining to measurements, that few persons agree as to the number of tiers or terraces on a side.

Poc cke, there in 1743, gives 260, the same as Lewenstein. Conder gives 206, and Greaves 207. Maillet, 208; Vausleb 255, and Bellonius 250. Lucas 243, Sicard (1711) 220, Davison (1763) 206, Ferguson 203, Dufeu 202 Prosper Alpinus (1591) 125. 208 seems to be the number generally agreed upon.

This difference is largely owing to the rubbish at the foot covering more tiers during some centuries than others; some sides being less perfect or more broken up; the top platform being smaller and higher, and, possibly, there being an actual difference on different sides.

On the top there is a level, the apex having been truncated. At least a portion of the loss of the upper corner has been by "wear and tear." Travelers who try to see how far out towards the base line they can throw a stone, or who send rocks hurling, crashing down the sides, have destroyed considerable. However, had there ever been either a marble-casing or common rock-corner stone it would have withstood the wear of the elements many thousands of years longer than it has. History tells us the marble was intact 8 or 900 years ago, but is not precise about the "chief-corner stone."

All the writers on the Great Pyramid seem puzzled over this platform at the top. It is rather more than 30 feet square, and hence is, and has been for ages, too large to be accounted for solely by removal of the corner stone, unless that were indeed a wonderful piece of marble.

The earliest writers describe the platform as much smaller than at present. Some declare it never had an apex. It has been compared in modern times, in view of the religious symbolisms of the interior, to be the "chief-corner stone which the builders rejected"—or the type of Christ.

It is rather a laborious task to reach the top, but most travelers do so, when a very remarkable view is thrown out before them. In the west the Libyan chain; to the southward, the Mokattam range; eastward, the quiet Nile passing along just as when Great Ramesis rushed his chariot along its banks; and all about, the wonderful "Field of Pyramids," with the tombs of the mightiest of earth.

Near by is the Sphynx, and but a few hundred feet off are the great brothers of the monument, but little smaller, and better preserved. On the northern face of the Great Pyramid the rubbish extends up the side from fifteen to sixteen courses of masonry. At forty-nine feet from the base, at the fifteenth or sixteenth course, on this north side, is an entrance into the interior. It is a small, narrow tube, three feet, five and one-half inches wide, and three feet and eleven inches high perpendicular to the *incline*. (Fig. 47). The opening has been badly mutilated, the masonry being torn out for a considerable distance. Strange feelings enter the soul as one enters this dark and silent passage. The bats and vermin, once prevalent, are now mostly driven away by the constant stream of

Fig. 47.

PARTS AND PROPORTIONS. 79

visitors; but in the earlier day, say in 1610, when Sandys entered, the pile of rubbish scattered within, and the dis-

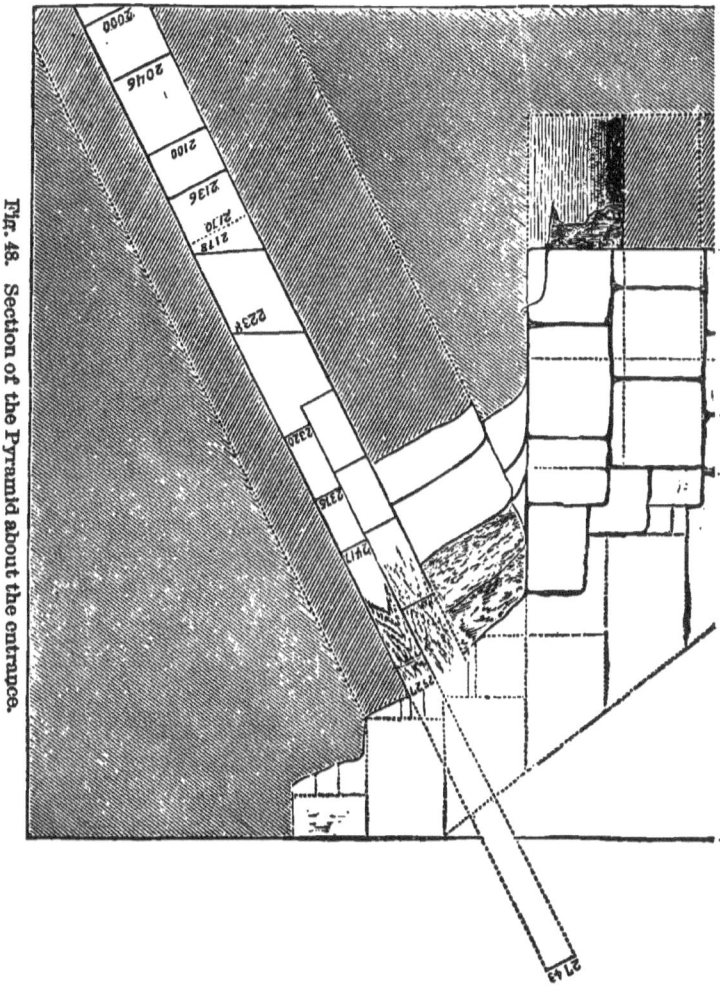

Fig. 48. Section of the Pyramid about the entrance.

gusting vermin, its inhabitants, made exploration decidedly unpleasant.

80 A GREAT MYSTERY.

Fig. 69. View of the entrance, dark square being the opening.

A very peculiar architecture is present at this opening—so peculi.r that we wish to call special attention to it. No writer has thus far mentioned the matter, and our conclusions may be wrong. An examination of Fig. 49, which represents the present appearance of the entrance, shows two pyramidal layers of masonry over the opening, the latter forming a square block beneath. By referring to Fig. 32, page 47, this will be found to resemble very closely, a portion of the names of Egypt. The hieroglyphs of Egypt possessed a greater significance in their language than we can now unravel, and we probably will never know the object of this form of ideation. It is worthy of note from the fact that it is the only structural mark on the building connecting it with the stone literature of Egypt. Almost every writer has claimed that beyond a few builder's daubs to guide the workmen, in unfinished chambers, the Great Pyramid was wholly free from hieroglyphs. This double layer of pyramid-arch over the entrance is not for the purpose of strength of structure, for the arch was unknown in Egypt for twelve hundred years after the Pyramid was built and a capstone covers the passage completely. Again, in the inner chambers there are flat roofs over large rooms. The narrow entrance does not require an arch, nor does this style of masonry represen ing a hieroglyph extend back over the passage any distance.

This entrance is not in the center of the pyramid, east and west, but removed some 24 feet and six inches to the east. The design of this deviation is unknown, unless it were to deceive those who searched for entrance during the ages it was sealed.

As we enter the narrow opening represented in Fig. 48, we find a passage of uncomfortable dimensions, extending southward and downward at an angle of 26° 41'. As this descending passage is now somewhat clear of rubbish, we can proceed without material change for a distance of 320 feet and 10 inches, when it becomes horizontal for 24 feet and 8 inches farther. At this point it enters a subterranean chamber. At least 23 feet have been worn and broken away from the mouth, so that its real length is not given. 4380 pyramid inches from the opening the ascending passage begins, the one which is blocked by the portcullis. The ang e of ascent is 26°18'. After passing upwards with no further deviation beyond the forced entrance of Al Mamoun, for a distance of 1542.46 inches, we suddenly straighten up in a long, lofty hall called the Gallery. It is from the junction of this ascending passage with the Grand Gallery that inch measures are taken, forward and backward towards the mouth, to represent the years of history. At present a few figures merely are given. By referring to Fig. 48, the highest number engraved in the passage is 2417, which implies that it is exactly 2417 inches from juncture of ascending passage and Grand Gallery. A little farther down are two lines vertical, and next, a dotted line at right angles with floor of passage. The dotted line is cut into the stone, and is supposed to represent the time of building the Pyramid, 2170 B.C. The other lines figured are joints in the masonry, every one of which has been most carefully measured by Prof. Piazzi Smyth. It will also be noticed in Fig. 48 that the layer of masonry on the side wall near mouth seems to be doubled up, backward, four inches below 2350, a subject to be referred to hereafter.

The subterranean chamber, which is 347 feet 10 inches from mouth of inclined passage, is a large gloomy vault 46 feet long, north and south, 27 feet and 1 inch wide, and 11 feet 6 inches high. From within it a shaft has been sunk to the depth of 36 feet, with no apparent result, its object probably having been to search for the supposed tomb of Cheops. This subterranean chamber is 99 feet below the base of the Pyramid, from base to ceiling. There is a continuation of the horizontal subterranean passage on the south side of th's chamber, extending 52 feet and 9 inches, where it abruptly closes. This chamber was entered some 60 years ago by Caviglia, with great difficulty. He found both Greek and Roman characters inscribed on the walls. The ancient writers declare it to have secret vaults hewn in the sides, but they were wholly imaginary. The location of the chamber is under the center of the Pyramid, but the center of the room is removed from the vertical axis about 2 feet and 11 inches east and west, and five feet north and south.

Reference to the plate at beginning of chapter (Fig.43) will show a long irregular passage descending from large hall or gallery referred to before, down to the passage leading to the subterranean chamber. This is known as the Well. By it any one could reach the interior of the Pyramid by ascent, without removal of the portcullis which rests in the ascending passage; or being in the upper passage, they could find their way out thus. It is a somewhat tortuous and disagreeable hole to penetrate.

At the point of junction between the descending and ascending passages, or rather where the floor line of the ascending passage would join the descending, (Fig. 50) is the point where measurements are taken for intersection. Immediately over, in the triangular space (B) descr.bed by dotted line, was the stone which once hid the portcullis from view. It mysteriously dropped out while the Arabs

84 A GREAT MYSTERY.

were pounding away at the masonry near by. But for this circumstance the interior would have remained sealed for ages.

The ascending passage rises at an incline of 25°49.22',

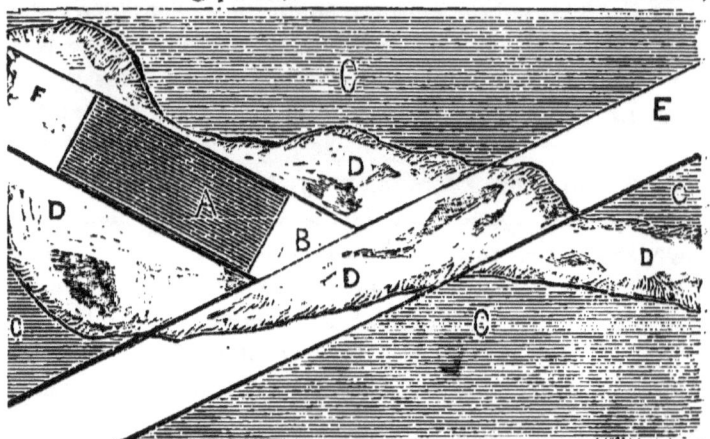

Fig. 50. Junction of the descending and ascending passages. E, the Descending Passage. F, Ascending Passage. D, Al Mamoun's Hole. A, Portcullis. B, Stone which fell. C, Masonry.

and is 1542.46 inches, or about 128 feet 6 inches to the Grand Gallery wall.

THE GRAND GALLERY.

The Grand Gallery is a long, narrow, high hall, ascending at the same angle as the passage. Its sides are made up of seven layers of masonry, each of which, as it rests upon the under one, laps over into the Gallery thus contracting its width near the ceiling. On each side of the floor of the Grand Gallery, extending up its entire length, is an elevation or solid stone bench, 24 inches high, and projecting out on the floor so that the entire breadth of Gallery of 82.12 inches is reduced, between the benches, to 41.2 inches, the benches being each 20.5 inches wide.

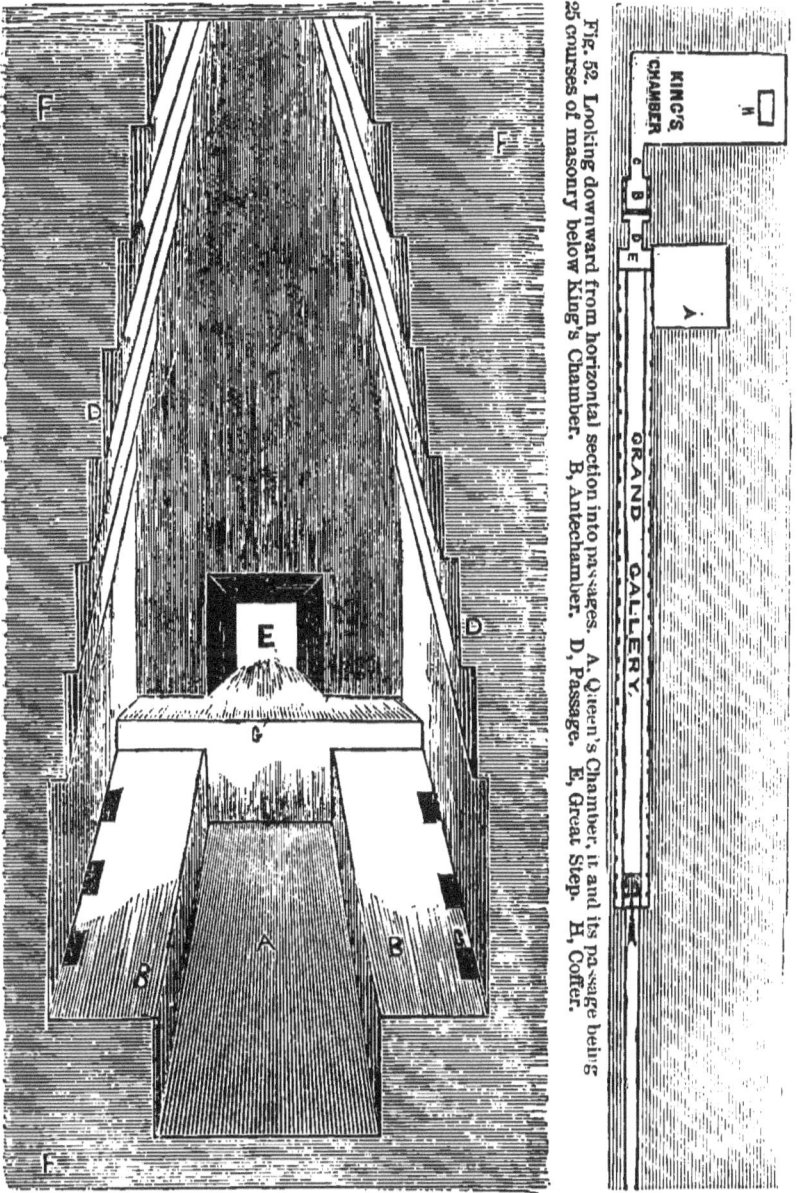

Fig. 51. Perspective view of upper end of Grand Gallery. A, Floor. B, Ramps or benches, showing three last ramp holes. D, Seven overhanging tiers of masonry. E, Antechamber. F, Masonry. G, Step to level floor.

Fig. 52. Looking downward from horizontal section into passages. A, Queen's Chamber, it and its passage being 25 courses of masonry below King's Chamber. B, Antechamber. D, Passage. E, Great Step. H, Coffer.

These benches are known as "ramps," and are composed of regular layers of stones. A perspective view of them can be had in Fig. 51, B, and plane in Fig. 53. The second stone, on the west—or right hand side entering, has been forcibly removed. It is known as the missing ramp stone. Figs. 52 and 53. In 53 an arrow is seen pointing downwards. This is the *mouth of the well*, and it is about 33 inches beyond the entrance or north wall of Gallery. To center of this missing ramp stone is 35.3 inches.

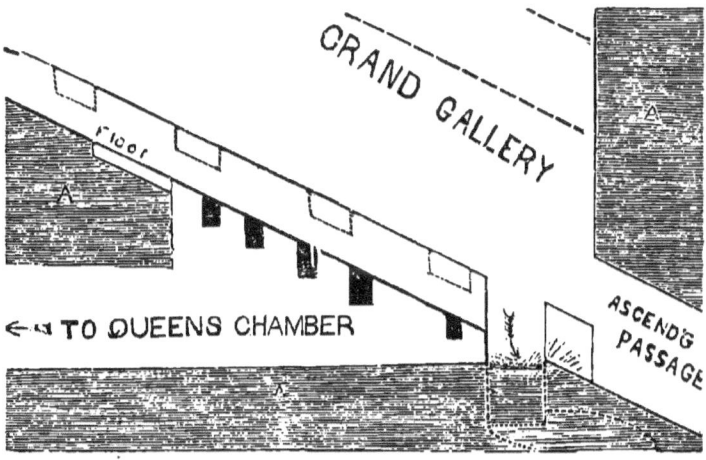

Fig. 53. North or Lower end of Grand Gallery, showing entrance of Ascending Passage, west side. In line with perpendicular wall is the first ramp stone. The second has been torn away to give entrance to Well; remaining rampstones are continuous, forming the west bench, showing the ramp holes dotted. The (black) cavities under the ramps, are "little graves" in the side of the junction of Gr. Gallery and passage to Queen's Chamber. A, Masonry.

The well descends irregularly to the long descending passage, uniting with the latter not far from the subterranean chamber.

For about 26 feet the well is perpendicular, (after a ragged *detour* from the missing ramp hole). It then becomes irregular again for 32.5 feet, when it opens out into an excavation, called the Grotto; from thence, down to the sub erranean passage it is irregular. The perpendicular, finished portion is a mystery—why should it be thus at such a place?

The removal of the ramp stone is also a mystery—and one to which there appears no reasonable solution. It was taken out with great *force*. So much so that the hard rock was split, portions still adhering to the remaining stones, on either side. Had it been removed by those on the inside after dropping the portcullis, it does not at once appear reasonable to suppose that they would put the stone in at all. During all the time the well was excavating, if built contemporaneous to the other passages, the ramp stone could either have been left out, or very smoothly and skillfully removed. Again, the finished, perpendicular portion shows that *time was* taken for the work.

There is one theory that comes to mind: Cheops builds the Pyramid for the scientific and religious objects indicated by symbolisms. He also places a tomb chamber deeply under it. But when death approaches, he finds that the universal hatred of the priests will not allow him to rest in peace. So he keeps his men secretly at work at the "well," hastens its completion, and is carried by his faithful friends after death to the upper chamber. They then sprung the mighty portcullis and creep out through the well.

This appears like very childish sophistry. Any one who sought his remains in the lower chamber could easily mount the same well by which the friends descended. To spring the portcullis was as easy a matter from the outside as from the inside—and save the trouble of making the well. There was also a heavy stone cemented in front of the portcullis to disguise its presence. What was the need then (with a well and with masonry to cover) of a portcullis at all? What is the meaning of a 26-foot portion being finished, ragged at both extremities? The key to this well is not yet in our hands.

Along the line where the floor of the ramps or benches meet the side wall of the Gallery, there are placed 28 mortices, or little excavations. What they are for is a riddle. A few insane reasons have been supposed, but not one that is worthy an instant's attention. If not symbolical, as hereafter represented—then they were doubtless placed there by chance, among the numberless "coincidences" some people imagine. The little mortices are called "ramp holes."

The height of the Grand Gallery is 339.6 inches, and the roof is formed of 36 overlapping stones. Its length, to a certain step, 36 inches high, (up to passage), is 1813+ inches. This step is 61 inches long. (See G, Fig. 51). But the length of the Gr. nd Gallery floor to where its line, continued through the step to the passage out of the gallery, is 1881.6 inches. We therefore speak of the Gallery as 1881.6 inches long.

The upper end of the Grand Gallery is very peculiar in its structure. Before reaching the south wall progress is interrupted by the vertical step, just referred to, which ri-es above the ramps or benches. (51-4-8.) This step, as mentioned before, is 61 inches on its horizontal plane before reaching the vertical of the south wall. It changes direction from the angle of the Gallery floor to a horizontal, and its continuation through the masonry leads into the antechamber, or room beyond. No architectural requirement calls for this step. It must mean something, and as the building, or passage, floor, roof, or walls did not demand it, its object must have been either symbolic or æsthetic. The latter it certainly is not; for a 3-foot step, interrupting the plan of construction, can hardly be called a thing of beauty? This step also hides or obscures one of the ramp holes—the 28th.

Another singular feature is that the south or upper end wall is not vertical. It "impends" or leans inward at an angle of 1°, so that the Gallery is longer in the center than on the ceiling. This also is required neither for beauty nor strength. This impending wall is also formed of overlapping stones, there being seven of them, between the step and the roof.

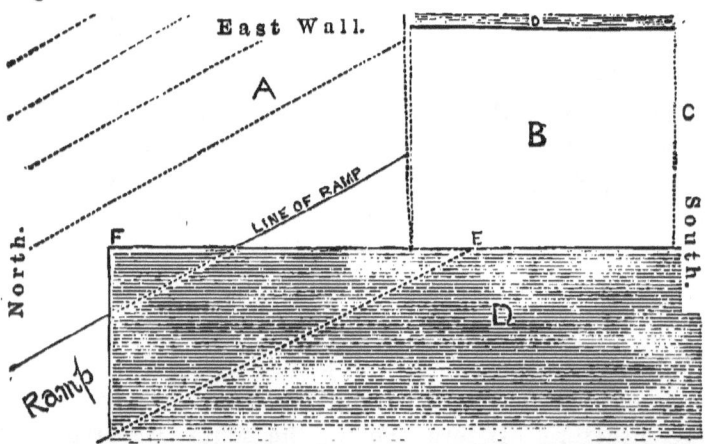

Fig. 54. D, Masonry. A, Upper end of Grand Gallery, dotted lines representing overhanging tiers of masonry on the side. B, Passage to Antechamber. C, Antechamber. E, Point where Floor of Gallery would intersect the passage floor. F, Corner of the Step. Dotted lines at head of Gallery represents the "impend" of the wall. East side.

The passage out of the Grand Gallery to the next room, the Antechamber, is 52.17 inches, or from beginning of great step, is 112.17 inches. It is 43.7 inches high, 41.4

wide. It opens into a room known as the Antechamber, a sort of waiting room to the King's Chamber beyond. The antechamber is 116.26 inches long, 149.3 inches high, and 62.5 inches wide. It is thus, except in height, merely an enlargement of the passage. But its interior is very peculiar.

On either side of the antechamber, as represented in Fig. 58, are four grooves, separated by small, narrow

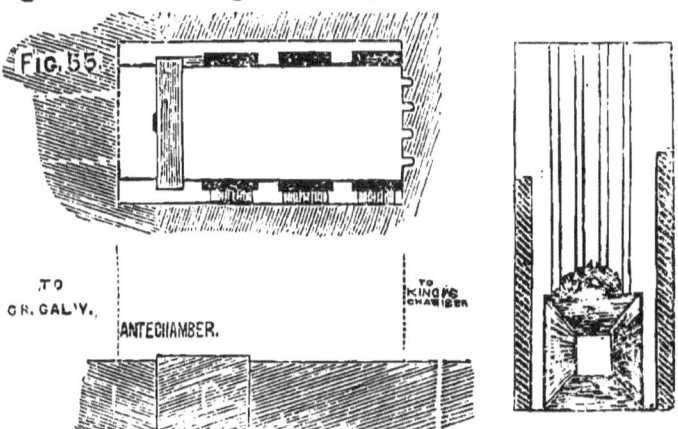

Fig. 56. Fig. 57.

Fig. 55. Horizontal section of Antechamber. Black portions on sides are the groove l sections. The dotted lines are the entrance. Opposite is the granite le for portcullis. The shade lines of masonry represent the change from limestone to granite.

Fig. 56. Masonry of floor of Antechamber, showing elevated stone and change from limestone to granite. Looking eas .

Fig. 57. Sou h end of Antechamb r, showing the four grooves, granite wainscoting, and passage to King's Chamber.

reliefs or pilasters. These grooves extend up the sides three-fourths of the height. They, and the ridges between them, constitute a sort of wainscoting of granite, making the room several inches narrower. They appear very much as if made to slide portculli in. The portion divided off next the north wall (K) is not grooved. In the second portion there is a portcullis, as it is called, though not resembling one in function or shape. (A). It is secure in its position, stretching across the room at the same height as the entrance passage, and consists of two slabs of stone, the upper and lower firmly joined. If it were dropped, then a person wou'd have to climb over it, but the entrance would not be occluded, there being 21 inches between it and the north wall. The three grooves (B), are now nearly obliterated by the barbarians, who hack at them for specimens. On the surface of this portcullis, or

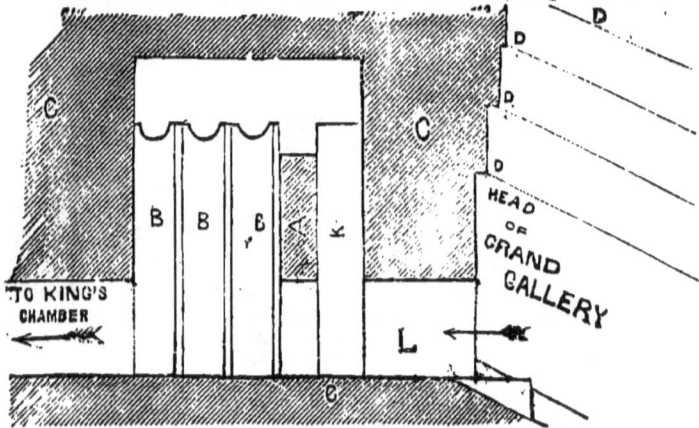

Fig. 58. The Antechamber and head of Grand Gallery. C Masonry. B, Grooves in side of antechamber. A, Leaf or Portcullis. D, Overlapping tiers of masonry in sides of Gallery.

"Granite Leaf," as it is called, next the entrance, is a projection, or relief sculpture. It is sometimes called an embossing, and very much resembles a crude "handle," like those placed at the end of heavy boxes, to lift. It is about 7 x 5 inches long and broad. The south wall also has four grooves, as in Fig. 57, extending from the entrance up to the ceiling. They are narrow, and divide the wall into five nearly equal ridges. The opening has

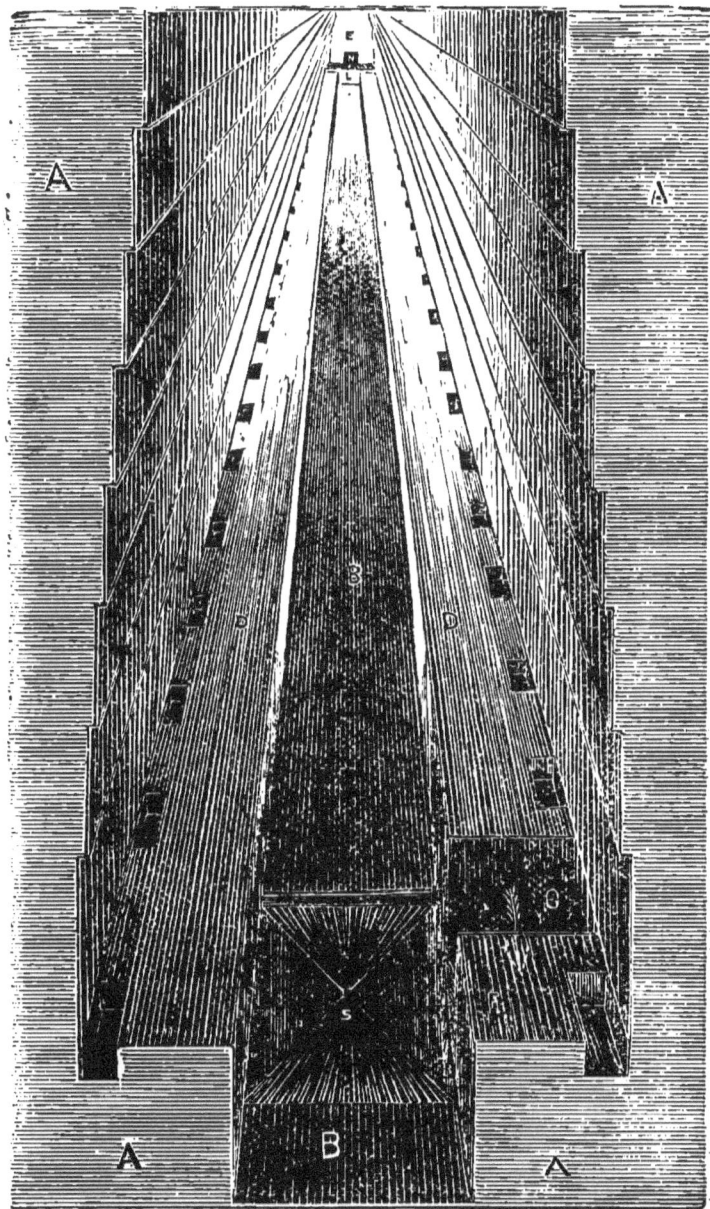

Fig. 59. Perspective of Grand Gallery, section at extreme north and lower end. A, Masonry. B B, Floor, interrupted by the horizontal passage, S, to Queen's Chamber. C, Missing Rampstone, arrow leading into the Well. D, Ramps or Benches. E, South Wall. L, Step. N, to Antechamber.

been considerably battered on its antechamber end. The north wall exhibits a rough, unfinished surface. It is composed of three massive stones.

The material of which the walls and general mass of the Great Pyramid are composed is limestone. But at this point, in the antechamber, we come in contact with a change for granite. This change appears to be methodical, and made with design to represent something—though *what*, is thus far undiscoverable. In the antechamber the floor is slightly raised for the distance of a single floorstone, (Fig. 56) where the granite begins. We do not keep a record of the changes from limestone to granite in the

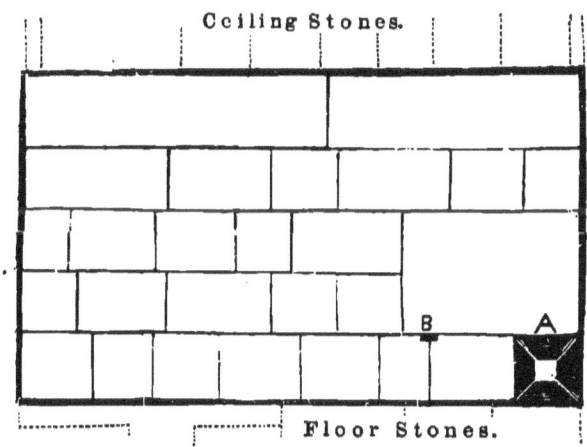

Fig. 60. North wall of the King's Chamber, showing the stones forming the five tiers. Junction of floor and ceiling stones shown. A, Entrance from Antechamber. B, Northern air channel.

construction, but they may be ascertained by following Prof. Smyth's three volumes on "*Life and Work at the Great Pyramid.*"

THE KING'S CHAMBER.

The passage out of the antechamber is a continuation

of that into it. It is 100 inches in length, 43.7 in height, and 41.4 in breadth. It opens into the King's Chamber, a large and lofty room, apparently the principal interior construction of the Pyramid. It is 412.13 inches in length, 206.3 in breadth and 230.1 high. Somewhat unlike the preceding room, it has no system of peculiar ridges, grooves or wainscots to vary the walls. They are very plain, smooth, polished, and exquisitely jointed. Its floor is on the 50th course of masonry from the base of the Pyramid. Its entrance is in the extreme lower, eastern corner of the north wall, as shown in Fig. 60. The surface of the walls and floor are very much marred by blows, scratches, marks and excavations. There are five tiers of masonry in the four sides, the upper tier being composed of very large, broad stones, the lower very much smaller. There are nine long stones stretching over it to form the ceiling, two of them at the extreme sides being only partially visible, as they extend over and beyond into the masonry of the sides. The joints, courses, and tiers of the King's Chamber have been a study, and enter largely into the mathematical relations of the building.

On the north and south walls are two openings—the two air holes for ventilation, orifices that extend from the King's Chamber to the outer world, as seen in Fig. 43. That on the north wall is only about 8x5 inches, while that on the south is near 17x23 inches. The latter, however, farther within the masonry narrows down to about the proportions of the other. The north air or vent hole is 233 feet long, and rises at angle of 33° 42'. The south hole is 174.25 feet long and rises at an angle of 45°.

Says Bonwick, "The King's Chamber is, in spite of the spoliations, a beautiful, granite-walled apartment. Noble slabs of granite, 20 feet high, and admirably joined, line the sides. The roof is flat. There is no furniture but the ever mysterious Coffer or sarcophagus." Greaves calls it a "rich and spacious chamber in which art may seem to have contended with nature." Again, it is called "a glorious room." It has been considerably mutilated in the attempt to find other chambers.

SARCOPHAGUS.

The only piece of furniture in the King's Chamber is a hollow rock. It is very finely dressed, and polished, and excavated. Its outside length is, (at mean of variations not extending over .5 of an inch on either side) 90 01 inches. Its height, also at a mean, is 41.27 inches. Its breadth is 38.65 inches. Its west side and lower surface are slightly curved. The average thickness of the sides is 5.99 inches, and the average of the bottom is 6.92 inches. It lies near the west side of the room, about the middle, north and south, and is slightly removed from a north and south position.

This lidless chest, coffer or sarcophagus, is made of porphory rock, and has been the bone of contention about the Pyramid for many years. Was it, or was it not a tomb? Many, and among them M. Jomard, have thought it too small for a sarcophagus, while others have thought it too large. It certainly is rather deep, and somewhat long for a modern coffin. Its history is appealed to in vain. There is no record worth noting of a body having been found within it. And yet there are sarcophagi in the tombs and pyramids of Egypt which resemble the coffer in the King's Chamber! But the same relationship to surroundings pertains to the entire Pyramid. Other pyramids are undoubtedly built purposely for tombs, but the most cursory examination of the Great Pyramid makes it extremely doubtful if it were ever a tomb—or at least if that were its primary mission. If other pyramids, with their sarcophagi, were built first, and the Kings of Egypt were in the habit of erecting such structures for burial, then, undoubtedly, the Great Pyramid was built as a tomb, with all its varied scientific accompaniments added thereto. But if the Great Pyramid were built first by an invading race, and the inferior giants of rock about it were subsequent imitations, then was the monarch of mounds built primarily for scientific objects, and used as a tomb secondarily, if at all.

One curious circumstance is notable, for it affects the theory that the use of the upper chamber, instead of the lower, for a tomb was on account of fear of disturbance after death. That is—the coffer must have been *built in* while the Pyramid was rising, for it is larger than the passage! Thus we see that during all the years of the building of the upper half, this coffer was in its chamber; and if a tomb, would it have been secret to the army of laborers? Imagine the singular questioning of the multitude constructing that interior, with two large "burial chambers" in it, when they had already run a shaft over 300 feet down into the living rock for the same object! It is not a satisfactory conclusion that this wonderful stone basin was ever a coffin. But many Arabian writers contend that the coffer did contain a body. Diodorus said: "Although these kings (Cheops and his brother) intended these for their tombs, yet it happened that neither of them were buried there. . . For the people being exasperated against them by reason of the toilsomeness of these works, and their cruelty and oppression, threatened to tear in pieces their dead bodies, and with ignominy to throw them out of their sepulchres: whereupon both of them, dying, commanded their friends privately to bury them in another place."—(Greaves).

There are evidences that it once had a lid, the remains

of grooves and pin-holes having been found. It was made of very resonant material, a blow from a hammer making a loud reverberating report. The vandalism of modern "ladies and gentlemen" has nearly destroyed its perfection and beauty by knocking off specimens to ornament some plaster Paris mantles among works of *virtu*. It should be a mark of disgrace in any parlor or cabinet to find such fragments, nicely labelled. We see the destiny of this noble urn which has rested since history's dawn in polished outline: It is to be scattered over the fire-places of civilized western hoodlums, who give the Arabs "bakhcesh" for their blows upon its edges!

The King's Chamber is not arched or vaulted. It has only a flat roof, and the immense mass of masonry above appears to be sustained by the great slabs of stone which stretch across. But in 1763 Mr. Davison discovered that directly over the chamber, and almost of equal size, was a broad low cavity left in the rock. The entrance to the room was through a forced passage from the extreme southeastern upper corner of Grand Gallery, as shown in upper left hand corner of Fig. 43. That this passage had been forced indicated that the chamber was for ages—and intended to be for years to come, a sealed room. In 1837, Col. Vyse, became convinced that there must be other resorts to remove superincumbent pressure than this single, flat room of equal size. He excavated upward along the east side of the ceiling, as seen in Fig. 61, and came successively to four more chambers; over the upper was a ridge roof of massive stones. The ceiling stones of the "Chambers of Construction," and King's Chamber are objects of interest. They are all of granite, even in the upper chamber. Those forming the ceiling of the King's Chamber are 326 inches long, 60 inches broad and

80 inches high. In all the chambers, especially the King's, they are highly polished and beautifully joined.

The most singular circumstance connected with the construction is that a design of some kind is evinced, beyond the matter of strength, in their method. The floor of each room is rough, unhewn. Yet the ceiling, which, as seen in Fig. 61, is not so high as the intervening stones themselves, is finely finished! In the second, third, fourth and upper chambers are quarry marks in hieroglyphs to guide the workmen in placing the stones. They are not cut in, but merely daubs of red paint. It appears to us that these five chambers, the last links of space, apparently, in the mighty monument, are of great significance, and deserve study; it is a matter of regret that so accurate an observer as Piazzi Smyth did not enter them, during his "Life and Work," and devote time to their thorough examination.

The names of these chambers of construction, beginning with the lower, are Davison's, Wellington's, Nelson's Arbuthnot's, and Campbell's. The upper, Col. Campbell's, has a "ridge" roof of eight "beautifully wrought" stones, which slope to each other at the peak.

The passage from Grand Gallery to Davison's chamber is 24 feet 9 inches long. From floor of King's Chamber to peak of Col. Campbell's chamber is 69 feet 3 inches. Davison's chamber is from 2 feet 6 in. to 3 feet 6 in. in height; Wellington's 2 feet 2 to 3 feet 8 inches; Nelson's from 2 feet to 4 feet 10 inches; Arbuthnot's from 1 foot 4 inches to 4 feet 5 inches; Campbell's from 5 feet 10 inches to 8 feet 7 inches in height.

Col. Howard Vyse found a piece of iron in the masonry which was transferred to the British Museum.

Fig. 61. View of Chambers of Construction from the south. East, or gable end view with Fig. 43. Irregular space to the left represents the excavation by which the chambers were discovered. A, Entrance passage into King's Chamber. B, air hole, and C the Coffer.

By the discovery of these Chambers of Construction a very important point was gained in the history of the Pyramid. Col. Howard Vyse, in 1837, discovered in the three upper chambers, on the faces of undressed stones, numerous hieroglyphics. They were red paint daubs, and demonstrated that there was a brush or pencil literature as well as stone literature at that time. Among these hieroglyphs were the cartouches of King Chofo, (Suphis, Shufu, or Cheops,) and Non-Chofo, (Nem-Shufu, or Sen-Suphis), the two brothers who are the supposed builders.

These ovals or cartouches are represented on page 29, Figs. 7 and 8.

These hieroglyphs confirm the statement made that the entire structure was kept free from hieroglyphs for some special reason. For these painted marks were undoubtedly to guide the workmen, and left in chambers closed, it was supposed, forever from human eyes. This shows that the whole building once had them for the same object. Their complete removal indicates that there was a *purpose* in their erasure. Nor do we have to look far for a legitimate purpose. It appears reasonable that there could have been but one object—to distinguish it in design, origin and theism from those monuments which do bear the imprint of the Egyptian chisel.

It is in these Chambers of Construction that many have hoped for a "Key" to the Pyramid. In view of their position—being the last known cavities in the chain; and the upward pointing of the higher chamber; the finished ceiling and rough flooring, indicating SOME purpose—these chambers should receive most critical attention. On the other hand, they have been conspicuously neglected. Their examination may yield a revelation. Even the upper passages were discovered by a *falling stone*.

PARTS AND PROPORTIONS. 103

THE QUEEN'S CHAMBER.

There is a horizontal passage which leaves the ascending, just a few inches within the Grand Gallery, and passes southward, vertical to the one just above it. Its origin is 23 inches from the north or lower end wall of the Grand Gallery; being therefore very near the missing ramp stone and entrance to well. (Fig. 59.) The King's Chamber, it will be remembered was on the 50th course of masonry. The Queen's, in like manner, floors or rests upon the 25th, yet to reach this 25th course its passage should start out from the ascending passage before reaching the Gallery. This however, did not seem to be in con-

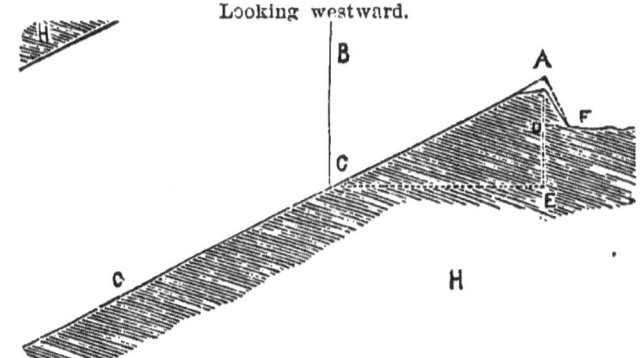

Fig. 62. Section of the beginning of the horizontal passage leading to the Queen's Chamber. (See Figs. 53 and 59.) G, Passage to Grand Gallery. B, Line representing the North wall of the Grand Gallery. C, Point where a plumb line from th : No th Wall s rikes the floor of the ascending passage. A, Place in floor where it sinks to F, the level of the horizontal passage. C to E 19.6 inches. E to D 0 inches. D to A 4.2, C to A 23.2 inches. A to F 4.7 inches.

sonance with the design of the builder. It leaves the ascending passage, as noted, within the Gallery, and at once sinks 4.5 inches, leaving a ridge and downward step, as seen in section in Fig. 62. It will be noticed by Fig. 59 and Fig. 53 (where masonry, A, begins between the ascending and horizontal passages) that the floor of the horizontal passage continues some distance before the roof begins—that is the floor of the Grand Gallery is cut away, so that a person in ascending the Gallery has to climb upon the ramps or benches to get up to the floor of the Gallery again. Or, they may by great exertion, if long limbed, put their feet in the "little graves," holes in side of this passage, and "straddle step" up to the fl or and climb upon it.

The total of the horizontal passage from north wall of Grand Gallery to Queen's Chamber is 1519.4 inches. At 763 inches is a small cylindrical hole in the floor, 8 inches in diameter, and 3 inches deep. At 945.3 inches is a hole in middle of the floor 4 inches in diameter and 4.5 deep. At 1122.5 inches, is a hole 3 inches in diameter, "filled with dirt,"—depth not given. At 1288 inches, a hole 2.5 in diameter.

At 1303.3 from north wall of Gallery, is a sudden change of level in the passage, the roof remaining the same. The descent is about 20 inches.

The height of this passage is about 46.5 inches until the change of level is reached, when it is near 68 (mean). Its width may be placed at 41.75 inches. The floor of this passage is, of course, limestone, of little value, and it is in an unfinished, unpolished condition.

As we enter the Queen's Chamber from the long passage, we find a large, ridge-roofed apartment, with walls of a fine species of white limestone. After visiting the Antechamber and King's Chamber, there is a feeling of disappointment in finding this room so inferior in finish. The floor is strewn with rubbish, the walls are less perfect, and there is a general impression produced that it is inferior in appointments to the grander chambers above.

It has more of the "dungeon" air about it. Its roof is ridged east and west, the ridge stones passing *one hundred inches* into the side wall. Its walls are here and there coated with a deposition of saline matter. This, to the chemist, is evidence of something we have never seen mentioned, and of a most unexpected nature—*moisture*. It is barely possible our observers have been deceived, but the frequent mention of the incrustations in the passage can leave no doubt as to the resemblance, if not actuality. Still, is it possible that in the heart of this mighty mass of rock, where dust falls like lead, that *mois-*

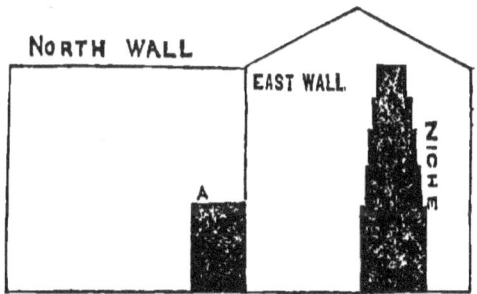

Fig, 63. Plane figure of east and no th walls of Queen's Chamber. A Entrance.

ture can exist in air—and if so, from whence? There surely must be some mistake, or else—either a rift in its massive sides or a cavity of water in the interior!

The dimensions are as follows:—East side 205.6 inches, West side 206 inches, South side 227.2 inches, North side 226.5 inches. Mean of the two sides:—East and West 205.8; North and South 226.7 inches. Mean of height, with ridge, 244.4 inches. Mean height to ridge 182.4 inches. The floor is much dilapidated, and appears to have been carelessly constructed. This does not confirm the opinion of a few who believe the Great Pyramid to have been built originally up to the 50th course only, (King's Chamber), and long afterward completed. For were this so, the upper and not the lower chamber would have been poorly constructed. That this room, amid such perfect work in halls and passages, should be so imperfect implies *design;* a design as yet beyond our ken.

In shape it is a heptagon—seven sides. The roof sides are 226.7 long,(same as sides), and 120.1 on the incline.

The most remarkable feature of the room is an immense niche in the east wall. This niche is a correct, and workmanlike excavation, as represented in Fig. 63 and 64, 185.8 inches high, and 61.3 inches wide at base. It narrows down to 52.3,—43.3—34.3—25.3 inches, successively.

Its depth is near 41 inches, backed by masonry which extends some distance into the Pyramid. At 38 inches above the floor a shelf runs across the niche, above which a hole or excavation extends back into the masonry some 100 inches, all badly marred by recent excavations.

The floor has been torn up and the masonry dug out, in several places, as seen in Fig. 64, all for investigation probably; possibly in search of buried treasure.

Another item in the Queen's Chamber already noted, is the fact of incrustations of a lime compound having formed on the walls and in the passage. It is well known that deposition of such salts cannot occur without moisture. How could moisture pertain to the atmosphere of this interior cavity? Could it soak through some vast rift in the sides—we must calculate on very rare and slight rains there. Can there be some hidden reservoir of water near by for scientific purposes? It seems extremely improbable. Nor is wonder lessened by finding no sign of incrustation in other passages. The ascending passage and the Grand Gallery are both open to the same

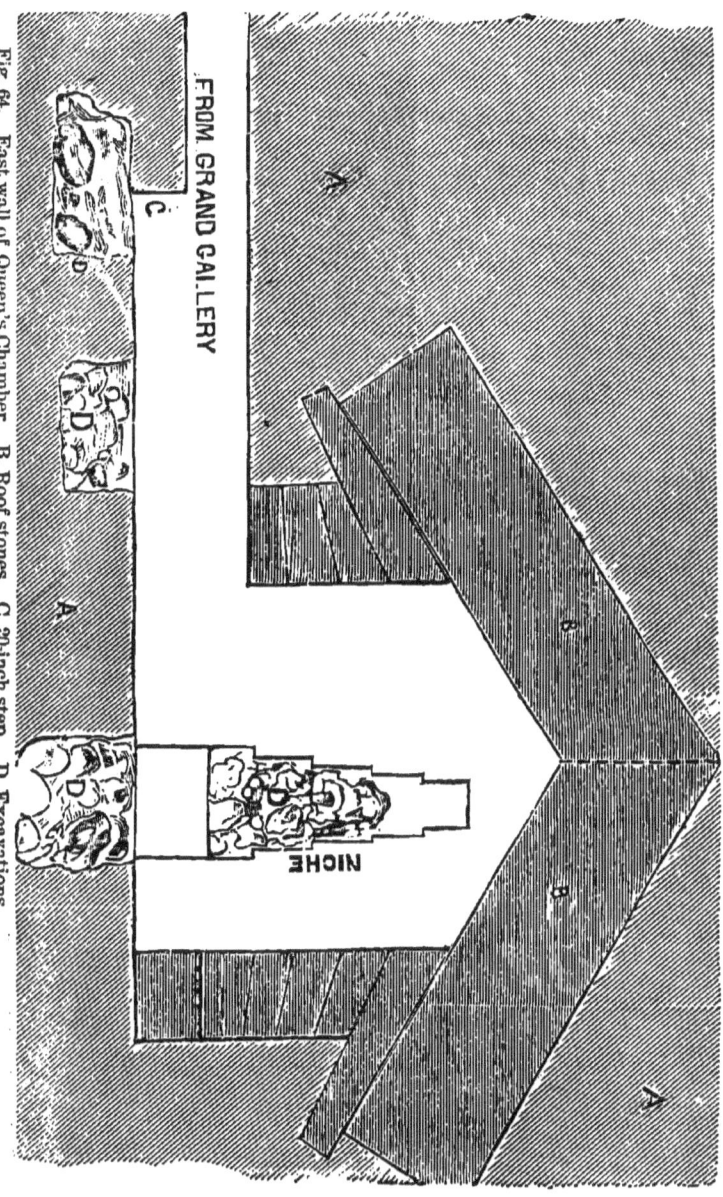

Fig. 64. East wall of Queen's Chamber. B, Roof stones. C, 20-inch step. D, Excavations.

influences, and both were closed by the same portcullis.

THE AZIMUTH TRENCHES.

"These azimuth trenches, then, are a sort of large open ditches, spread about here and there on the surface of the hill before the eastern face of the Great Pyramid; and not very noticeable, except for their relative angles in a horizontal plane; for these gave me the idea, at first sight, of being strangely similar to the dominant angles of the exterior of the Great Pyramid."—(*Smyth*).

There remains one thing more in "Parts and Proportions." It is supposed that a hidden chamber exists in the Pyramid, the discovery of which will throw light upon its meaning and mission. Among the various causes for this belief the symbolic is the greater.

At one place on the Pyramid hill are a multitude of chips of Black Diorite rock. No tomb in the hill, or discovered portion of the Pyramid, is built of this stone excepting a small place in the descending passage. Hence it is supposed the undiscovered chamber is lined with it.

This supposition is not unreasonable when we remember how closely the Pyramid itself was sealed, and how the entire upward channel was portcullised, and then the portcullis hidden by masonry.

Fig. 65.

THE MOTIVE.

Before taking up the analysis of the scientific and symbolic character of our subject there is a point worthy of close attention. It is possible, even extremely probable, that in some manner the Great Pyramid was built as a tomb. But a tomb could have been built with great elegance of design or with great simplicity, and still had no deviations from a complete, harmonious, and distinct plan. However crude in art or barbaric the artist—however lithe in design or cumbrous in conception, the effort is always to symmetry. The failure to attain symmetry may be complete. The curved lines may be monstrosities, the angles unfortunate—but the effort is there, and the proportion, also, though perhaps a very poor one. Thus, if the builders of the Pyramid designed a tomb with various chambers, and a heavy stone coffin, and finely built passages, it was not a difficult matter to build it. Labor and stone were in plenty. That they should have built such a tomb in certain measurements which represented many of the more modern and sublime problems in mathematics was singular, very singular. Yet the student is forced to admit that a few relations of feet to figures may have been coincide ces. The universality reduces the probability, but still the possibility remains. Also, with regard to certain linings on the walls at such distances as would represent dates, or with proportions of size which give astronomical truths, they *may* all have been coincidental.

There may have been no *motive* in these relations. The very "starting point"—that is, the taking accidentally of a certain angle as the basic proportion, may have induced the subsequent measurements. But no one will believe it did so happen.

This is the lame position taken by a few Pyramid students. Their number is daily lessening. It is true that the coincidental may, amid a thousand million chances, have ruled the progress of its erection in the purely figurative expression of its volume and contents.

But in morphology there are no coincidences. There must be a motive. Not a leaf figures its microscopic shape but from motive in a physical sense. A child cannot whittle a stick without having in mind some contour to produce. There are parts of the mighty Pyramid which never could have been introduced without a *motive*. We pass by the angles, the star angles of descent and ascent— the portcullis, its singular scaling—the well, its partly finished condition, etc. First, the benches or ramps: If they could have had a design in accordance with the physical operation of building, how is it with the ramp-holes? But supposing these to have been required, we come then to that ugly, ill-proportioned step, three feet high, and 60 inches long, right where a step is to be avoided. Could this obstacle be placed there without a *motive?* And if a motive, what could it have been but to represent something for whosoever unearthed it in future ages? Take next the granite leaf in the Antechamber. It is a couple of heavy stone strips, finely joined, stretched across a room just where it could possibly have no architectural object. It has been called a portcullis. The foolishness thereof is inexpressible. If it *could* slide, it would interrupt no passage. But it cannot, for it rests at either end, in the

THE MOTIVE.

sides of the room, on good solid granite. And what of the relief sculpture like a handle, on it? A 7 inch handle in the Pyramid? We might mention the slight elevation so cleanly cut in floor of Antechamber, and other equally singular features. These all point to a motive, and place the interior construction of the Pyramid far beyond the coincidental, for these elements are only factors in a grand whole, and whatever may have been the motive for the great step, was the motive also for the thousand singular proportions which a few hardy disputants relegate to the coincidental.

It is not claimed that the motive of the building is yet discovered, but multitudes of the details have been appropriated, and those, in a measure, we will try to represent.

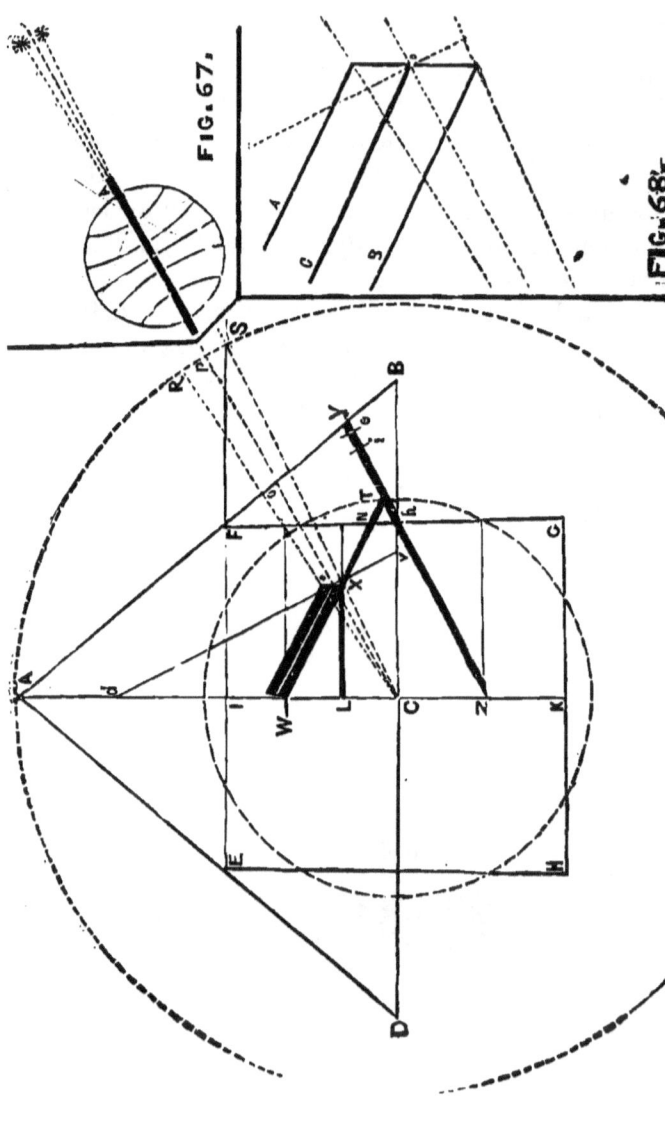

Fig. 66. A B D, the Pyramid angles. A C, the vertical. D R, the base. E F G H, a square of equal area, having its centre at the centre of the Pyramid's base, C. If the square I F C h be trisected at W and L, then W will represent the level of the King's Chamber, and L, the level of the Queen's Chamber. C S represents the lower culmination of the pole star, by a line drawn from centre of base. C R, upper culmination. C p, the actual pole. Fig. 68 shows how these lines intersect the north end of Grand Gallery on a larger scale. A being the roof, B the floor, and C the graven line on centre of wall. v d pointed to Alcyone and intersected the graven line. (Seen in 68). Fig. 67 shows the relation between the polar axis and the two positions of Draconis.

SYMBOLIC ANALYSIS.

CHRONOLOGY.

T is confidently asserted that the Channels of the Great Pyramid represent the important events in history; but more particularly the varied course of that great stream of theosophy which originated in the earliest epoch, and subsequently became the mission of the Jewish race—to perpetuate until the time of Jesus Christ.

We now come to the most remarkable series of scientific demonstrations of a religious proposition that the philosopher has ever pondered over. Never before has science been made the exponent of religion. Never has prophecy held the reigns over positive philosophy, as she thus holds mathematics as a factor in the demonstration of the religious symbolism of the Pyramid. The great proposition upon which the Chronology of the Pyramid is based is that the *inch* represents a year. This is the basis of its mystery of prophecy.

The basis for this proposition is startling in its distinctness. It is three, four—even six fold in its application:—

The longest measurement in the Pyramid in inches,

is equal to the longest measurement of time in the universe, as known to us. The longest measurement is the diagonal of the base. The base surface is a square having 9131 inches on a side and its diagonal is consequently 12,913.34 inches. There are two of these diagonals, and together they make exactly 25,826.68 inches. (Fig. 70.)

Is there any thing remarkable in this number? There are two years known in the measurement of time. One, the solar year, is the revolution of the earth about the

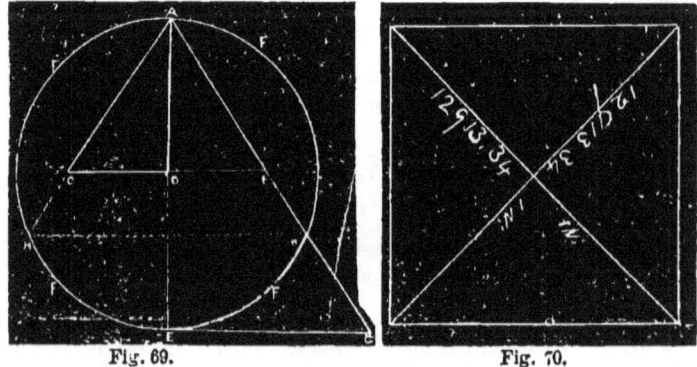

Fig. 69.   Fig. 70.

Fig. 69. A, B, C, Portion of the Pyramid above floor of King's Chamber. A, H, H, The entire Pyramid. A, D, Vertical, which is a radius of 4110.5 inches. Continued to E is the diameter of the circle F, 25,826.68 inches in circumference. C, D, is also one side of a square, (6456.75 inches), the four sides of which equal 25,826.68 inches.

Fig. 70. Square base of the Pyramid, 9131 inches on a side, and two diagonals of 12913.34 inches each.

sun. It takes 365.242 days for the circuit. But the longest measurement of time known to us is the "Precessional Cycle." This is the revolution of the whole starry host about an *apparent* axis, the star Alcyone, of the Group Pleiades. This is observed by the fact that the stars rise about 50 seconds *later*, each year. For this complete circuit of the heavens, (apparently around Alcyone), and the close of the cycle, it requires just 25,826.68 years. Singular that the longest linear agrees with the longest circle time—count'ng inches for years? One relation of this kind may be coincidental. In this problem just given we present the evidence of the dominant or principal square in the Pyramid, its two diagonals giving the above result; each diagonal is, of course, the hypothenuse of a *triangle*, and the result may be called the demonstration of the triangle.

Jas. French says:—"We would look, however, for the demonstration of a circle, in a problem involving the revolution of the heavens." On the level of the King's Chamber, at the 50th course of masonry, this is secured.

It will hereafter appear that this level is an important point for measurements, giving ample reason for looking to it for the solution of such a problem. The discovery was made by Prof. Hamilton L. Smith, of Geneva, N. Y. The height of the Pyramid, above the level of the King's Chamber floor is 4110.5. This is the radius of a circle which is equal in measurement to the perimeter of the square at the point of truncation—that is, the surface of the base of a pyramid, cut off at the floor of the King's Chamber, (or the top surface of the truncated pyramid left when it is removed,) is 6456.67 on a side.

We mention this to show that this radius (the 4110.5) is not taken hap-hazard, but of all radii presented, is *the* one to be chosen—the radius producing a circle equal to the base of a pyramid whose vertical it is. This radius of 4110. 5 doubled for a diameter and multiplied by 3.14159 to get the circumference, = 25.827 inches, the length of the precessional cycle. This is the demonstration of a *circle*.

Now among the dominant measurements of the Pyramid, as already mentioned, is the level of the King's Chamber floor. On the outside of the square, each side gives 6456.67 inches. The four sides give, as before, the consummation of the greatest cycle of time—exactly 25,826.68 years are required. Is it singular that the longest linear of the Pyramid should agree with the circle of 25.827 inches? This is the demonstration of the *square*.

Thus the testimony of the triangle, circle and square evidences the time values of linear measures in the Pyramid.

There are other propositions which indicate that the inch may represent a year. For instance, a certain mark in the wall in the descending passage is at such a distance in inches from the north wall of the Grand Gallery, that 412.55 inches (length of King's Chamber) added to it, will give the precessional number 25,827.

These demonstrations of the relation of length to time are greatly strengthened by the time data of other parts of the Pyramid, as given on another page. For instance, the base of the Pyramid is a number of which the days and the fraction of a day in a year is a factor together with the ancient sacred cubit. (365.242x25=9131).

Supposing it to be fairly demonstrated that an inch linear represents a year, the next step is equally difficult to establish,—where shall the era of the world's history begin? And when the starting point is found, the great events of history must correspond exactly with it. Thus, with the above inch-year demonstrated; a reasonable starting point proposed; and the greatest events of time filled into the various niches,—it is not difficult to believe the chronological import of the Pyramid. If a person were called upon to state what event had modified and controlled the current of history, antecedent and subsequent, more than any other—be he theist or atheist—there could be but one answer. The world's hopes, as developed and "chrysalized" in every known religion, looked forward to a

CHRONOLOGY. 117

Prince in the religious sphere who was to redeem humanity. Every war for 18 hundred years has turned upon the Birth of Christ, or been modified by the creed of his Church. Every political intrigue, and every national constitution is shadowed by the cross or crescent, both of which proclaim Christ the "Greatest of Prophets."

This is the one event which has universally modified history, *both antecedent and subsequent*. It may be either the Birth or *Death* of Christ. Whatever may be our belief in reference to the mission, the historical importance of his appearance is paramount. From a religious standpoint the Birth is recognized as the beginning of the era, from the fact of prophecy pointing to that time, and the "star in the east" then appearing. From a purely historical standpoint its importance is testified by the beginning of a new chronology in Christendom.

The point selected on general principles to represent the Birth of Christ is the north wall of the Grand Gallery. This selection is borne out, first, by its "fitting" other events and marks; and, second, by a peculiar astronomical proof.

During the 25,827 years of the precessional cycle the pole star, or nearest pole star, changes. At or about the supposed date of the building of the Pyramid the pole star was a Draconis. This star, however, was $3°42'$ away from the real pole of the heavens, and the revolution of the earth about its axis would make it appear sometimes $3°42'$ above, and again $3°42'$ below the real polar point, a difference of $7°24'$. Inclination of the earth's axis being $30°$, the upper culmination of Draconis was $33°41'24''$. Its lower culmination was $26°18'10''$.

This lower culmination is very nearly the line of the descending passage. If a line be drawn as from C to S,

(Fig. 66) from the base center of the Pyramid toward Draconis at its lower culmination, S, it will pass through the intersection of floor and north wall at the extreme lower and northern point of the Grand Gallery,(on a surface "elevation," as in the figure). Another line drawn from C to R, towards Draconis at its upper culmination will pass through the intersection of the roof and north or lower end of Grand Gallery. Now this may be taken as evidence that the beginning of the Grand Gallery was an important point in the Pyramid measures. But to make it still more important, or to indicate that this position of the Grand Gallery was not accidental, if we draw a line from C to the exact north pole of the heavens, parallel to the earth's inclination it will pass through the end of the Grand Gallery midway from floor to roof—and at this point a long line, extending the full length of the Gallery is graven in the rock! This line is 1878.4 inches long; in relation to the symbolisms of the Gallery it may indicate the beginning in 1878 of the influence of the great perihelia of planets in 1881, a most remarkable astronomical "landmark."

This evidence of the importance of the North end of the Grand Gallery is not complete, however, until a line is drawn on the plate, from V to d, intersecting X and pointing to Alcyone, the star around which the precessional cycle occurs. It will also intersect the graven line at the same point as the 30° line from C to P.

Another prominent reason for taking the north wall of Gallery for Birth point of Christ is the following:

From the north wall down to the ascending passage to junction of descending, up descending, a total distance of 2170.536 inches, is a line graven in the wall of the *passage*, se n at *i*, Fig. 66. If the length of the King's Cham-

ber be added to this (412.132 inches) the total is 2582.-
668 inches, just one tenth of the precessional cycle.

The great value of this incident is that the number
25,826.68 could not bear a relation to so many measurements without design.

Admitting that the location of zero in our chronology
is at the north wall, and every inch is equal to one year,
let us see what dates are recorded:

Down ascending passage to floor junction of descending passage, (Fig. 71), from H to I is 1291.2 inches, H
to O is 1482, H to L 1542. From C, (the axis line of pas-

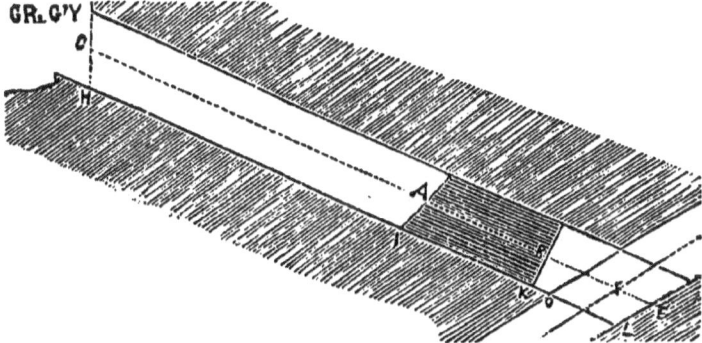

Fig. 71. Measurements at the junction of the passages from the north
wall of Grand Gallery. C, A, B, F, E, Axis of ascending passage—which
is shortened in the figure. Upper end of Portcullis as at present chipped
away.

sage) to F is 1532.8, and to E is 1562.8 inches. We
would take the dominant measure to be the floor line
from H to L. These are English inches excepting from H
to L, which are Pyramid inches.

Now these dates must be B. C., and 1542 is the supposed date of the "Burning Bush," at which time Moses
received his first mission to take the children of Israel
out of Egypt. 1482 is very nearly the date of the Exodus.
Thence passing up the descending passage to the extreme
point of the present floor—or to where it met the layer

of rock which back.d the ca-ing stones, we reach 2527 inc' es, which is represented as the "Dispersion," or the breaking up of the human race into different nations. Although these dates are far from being well established, and fall short of the demonstration given to the inch-year proposition, still one or two quite remarkable incidents have occurred in discovering them.

Mr. Casey, a Pyramid student of great application, wrote to Prof. Smyth that if these passages were chronological they certainly would have some mark to indicate its own erection. And as the date of the erection had been almost positively fixed at the beginning of the precessional cycle in 2170 B. C., Mr. Casey added, "According to this theory [inch-year] that date must be three or four hundred inches down inside the top or mouth of the entrance passage. Is there any mark at that point?"

The Astronomer Royal hastened to his notes, computed the distance, and lo! There graven in the wall, on either side, was a line *perpendicular to floor of passage*, as seen in Fig. 48, 2170 inches from the Grand Gallery! No one will be so foolish as to suppose *chance* engraved these lines!

The next feature after the birth of Christ, or the north wall, is the Crucifixion, and just 33 inches up the Grand Gallery is the mouth of the Well, descending down into the Subterranean Chamber, or the grave. The analogy is carried still farther by the forcible removal of the ramp stone to get to the well, (p. 87). There are many features about this Gallery that are appropriated for symbols of the Christian dispensation. Some of them are exceedingly imaginative. The ramp holes being open, are designated as graves, open because Christ has opened them by his death. Against each ramp hole in the wall is set a finely cut stone of certain height. This is represented as symbolizing the flight of the soul. The size of the ramp holes is 8 by 7 inches. Seven is, in mystic numbers, the sign of the consummation, and eight refers to new life! The seven tiers of overlapping stones, either side, are referred to the seven churches of Asia. The 36 roof-stones are supposed to represent the 36 months of Christ's ministry, extending over the entire period of the Christian dispensation.

Whatever may be the future of the Pyramid's chronology, at present it is an exceedingly tangled thread, with here and there a gleam, in the shape of some date which fits the space, but probably removed from all its connecting links.

There are strong analogies, but in a study of unsustained data, liable to error, and not necessarily attached to our subject. Especially is the upper end of the Grand Gallery, with the 3-foot step, made to yield a multitude of concidences connected with the advancement of civilization, religion, and human freedom during this latter day Probably the most important part is the nature of the "impending wall" at the north end, and the narrow passage beyond, which symbolizes the closure of the great present epoch, and *end of the age*,—though not the end of the world. In continuation of this idea the King's Chamber represents the second coming of Christ. The narrowing of the Grand Gallery into the passage to Antechamber signifies great tribulation to fall upon the earth from 1881–2 to 1886. As this is the age of the great planetary perihelia, the probabilities of its correct prophecies seem startling indeed.

CHRONOLOGICAL NOTES.—The length of the Grand Gallery on the graven line, is 1878.4 years or inches. (Fig.

72.) The Evangelical Alliance was formed at that time.
The length of Grand Gallery on the floor, from the
north wall to step at A, is 1812.986 inches. The base
measure of the Pyramid, 9131.05 inches, divided by five*
is equal to 1826.21, which reaches to R, on an imaginary
continuation of floor line. R is 13.224 from A. This is
also the distance from L to M. The full Gallery length,

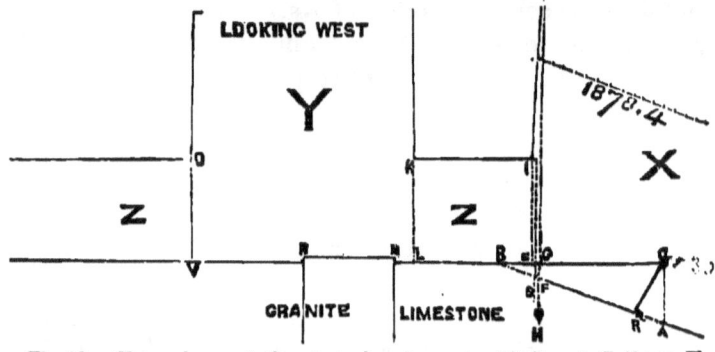

Fig. 72. Chronology of the Antechamber, etc. X, Grand Gallery. Y,
Antechamber. Z, Passages. H, Plumb line showing the impend of south
wall of Grand Gallery.

1878.4—1826.21=52.19. This is also the length of the
passage E to L, or I to K. The coincidence indicates some
significance in the date.

The north wall of the Antechamber is rough, unfinished.
The other sides are finely finished. This indicates that
the north wall is not used for the same purposes as the
others, and we naturally take it to be chronologically mis-
placed. This displacement is put at 55.74 inches, or
this reason: The entire length of the Antechamber is
116.26 inches. From M to N, the first granite block, the
floor is raised 3-10ths of an inch. The north wall being
displaced, it is natural to connect this raised stone with its
correction. From N to V is a distance of 55.74. If the

---

*Five is what is called a "Pyramid number." That is, five enters into its
construction so often as to call attention thereto. It has five sides. The
King's Chamber is on the 50th course of masonry; the Queen's is on the
25th. The King's Chamber has five tiers of masonry in its walls, so placed
with great precision. Various other instances are noted.

south wall (v) be brought forward to N, the displaced wall will reach to s, 3.55 inches into the Gallery, leaving a wall over 3 inches thick, from s to where the Gallery wall would be if vertical, (the line F).

We differ somewhat from this view. The granite elevation would extend to L if the explanation be— that the entire Antechamber was to be moved. The south wall would then also be roughened. The elevation indicates that both M and N have an import. The extreme end of the entrance passage (Fig. 48) is 2527 inch-years from the north wall. 55.74 inches added to it gives the precessional cycle, within a small error, as obtained by 2170+ 412.132, (p. 116). The latter equation shows that nearly 56 inches more are required in the channel line. From N to V supplies the deficiency. But how about the displaced wall? From L to M is 13+inches. If the unfinished L were placed at M, against the elevation and the beginning of the granite, what displacements would it correct? It would put G over B, where it architecturally belongs! And chronologically it would bring A to R, in accordance with the note on page 122.

Several recent works on chronology unite upon 4104 B. C. as the limit of man's history. The 6000 years of the Bible would then terminate in 1896. The Gallery floor to A gives 1812.986 years, and computed to B, 1896.1785.* B is the north and south *vertical center of the Pyramid.*

2582.668, the precessional cycle in tenths, added to the width of the King's Chamber, 206.066,=2788.734, the time set by Prof. Smyth, astronomically, for the Flood.

25,826.68 inch-years, the great cycle, divided by 25, (the number of inches in a sacred cubit)=1033.0672; the 1000 years are symbolical, and the odd 33.0672 equals 33 years, 24 days, and 13 hours, the time of Christ's ministry on earth. Single coincidences are slight evidences, but two distinct and separate coincidences in the same problem, pointing to the same conclusion, show that somewhere in the mazes is a thread connecting and corroborating them. Hence this relative coincidence has a value: 116.26 inch-

---

*This measurement to A and from A to B has since been modified so that B represents 1894.

years, (length of Antechamber) — 83.1925, (the inch-years from A to B) also = 33.067 +.

The chronological import of the Queen's Chamber and its passage, is involved in even greater doubt than the upper channel. Some writers believe its rough, horizontal plane and rugged outline represents the career of the Jews, as distinct from Christendom. We will suggest that if the modern theory of identity between the lost ten tribes of Israel and the Anglo Saxon race be true, that the diverging channels, which deviate at the symbol of the death of Christ, represent the history of both branches of the great Semitic race.

It is objected that their history could not be contemporaneously represented by passages which differ in length.

Mr. Thomas Wilson, a prominent and careful Pyramid student, claims* that the horizontal passage goes 25 feet beyond the vertical axis which strikes the upper passage

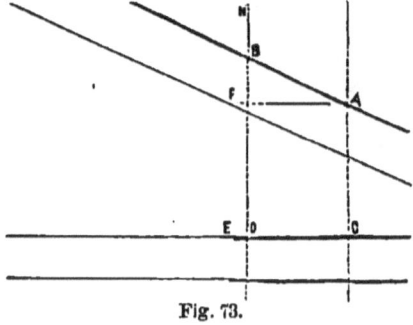

Fig. 73.

at B, Fig. 72. But he a'so states that the year-space in the lower passage is 1.115 inch s instead of one inch. We presume this is represented in Fig. 73. A B is a line on the incline. The same distance carried horizontally will extend to F, or C D becomes C E. Hence, the horizontal passage must be longer contemporaneously.

But is it true that the inch year should be lengthened? If modified at all should it not be *shorter* on the horizon-

---

*"Our Rest," June, 1879. A journal devoted to Pyramid study. Thomas Wilson, Publisher, Chicago.

tal? Does not the horizontal inch extend .115 farther into a chronologically constructed *whole Pyramid* than the inclined inch—and therefore compass too much? On the other hand, is not the modification of the inch in any direction destructive of the very process by which the inch-year is established? This change of values also requires alteration of the time measures on the plane of the Antechamber. Still again, the vertical axis is not a factor, justly, in this mensuration, when it passes many feet to the west without intersection. Even though it did intersect, its point on the passages is a matter of dispute between Jomard, Vyse, Wilkinson, Smyth, etc. It is possible that the termination of the horizontal passage may represent the end of the Jewish wanderings, and restoration to their own land, Palestine.*

THE FLOOD.—If our race were nearly or quite destroyed by a Flood in ages past, the Pyramid would certainly record it. Prof. Smyth has reasoned from certain physical and astronomical data that the Flood occurred 2800 B.C. Bishop Usher's Biblical chronology gives it 2349 and other versions 3246 B.C. The mean of these is 2797. The Pyramid has a significant feature which points directly to this event. As already noticed, the entrance passage is too short by nearly 56 inches to chronicle the Great Year of the Pleiades. Then it is too short to denote the Flood. But for some reason the masonry at the outer end is *doubled* upon itself. (Fig. 48). This fold is 216 inches, which added to the outer end, 2527, gives 2743—the year of the Deluge—the beginning of the history of the present inhabitants of the earth.

ASTRONOMICAL RELATIONS.

The entrance angle of the Great Pyramid is such that in the year 2170 B. C. the then North Star *a* Draconis,

---

*Recent political and meteorological conditions point to this with startling distinctness: The close of the prophetic season of tribulation; the decay of the Ottoman Empire; the imperial influence of D'Israeli on the Eastern Question; the past due mortgages which the Rothchilds hold on Palestine, which the Turkish Government does not attempt to pay; the great change in the climate of Palestine, rainfalls being again abundant, and her vineyards bl oming as of old—all are "signs" of an approaching change in Jewi h h story.

shone directly down its dreary length—to the subterranean Chamber. No other light than the dim radiance of "The Dragon" ever penetrated it. At the same time, 2170 B. C., the axis star of the heavens, Alcyone, shone brightly over the apex. This occurs, as indicated before, once in 25,826.68 years. Alcyone was the Greek "Halcyon,"—happy star. As Alcyone was Queen of the Pleiades, their "sweet influences" (Job) were peculiarly the Great Pyramid's benediction. This year, (2170 B. C.), the year of the Pyramid's erection, confirmed by the graven line in descending passage, was known in astronomy as the "Great Year of the Pleiades."

Sun's Distance.—The angle of the Pyramid's sides is such that for every nine inches of vertical the side measurement is 10. Also the diagonal of the base, given in Fig. 70, bears the same relation to the sides. Now the vertical height of the Pyramid, 5813 inches, multiplied by 10 raised to the 9th power equals 5,819,000,000,000 inches, which are equal to 91,840,270 miles, the correct distance of the sun from the earth!

Regarding this figure, there has been much discussion in the astronomical world. When the sun's distance from us was first given by astronomical computation, the received opinion of the *savants* was 95,000,000 miles, and the former estimate received no little ridicule. The latter number had even been increased by what were then recent calculations. A writer in "*Our Rest*" compends the history of "sun science" as follows: "The ancients estimated the distance of the sun from the earth at 10 miles;* it was increased afterward to 10,000 miles; then it ran up to about 2,500,000; it then took another leap to

---
*He might have said "the ancient Egyptians," for such was the case until more than a thousand years after the Pyramid was built.

some 36,000,000; early in this century it reached 95,000-000 miles; then it decreased to 91,500,000 miles; again it increased to 92,500,000, [most astronomers put it at 95,-000,000]; now it is estimated at 91,840,000 miles." No common language will describe the thrill which electrified Pyramid students when the extensive and expensive observations recently taken of the "transit of Venus,"—observed in every part of the world—gave the astoundingly parallel result of 91,840,000 miles. This is just 240 miles from the Pyramid estimate—with a parallax of 8.879 seconds of a degree? The *Les Mondes*, of Paris, truly remarked, "The Great (*Grande*) Pyramid has conquered?"

Not only does the Pyramid give the sun's distance, but it gives very precise data regarding the earth's size, specific gravity, etc. The distance of the sun is obtained, as mentioned, by multiplying the vertical of the Pyramid by 10 raised to the 9th power. If this result, 91,840,270, be divided by twice the vertical of the Pyramid we get 7,899.56, which in miles is the exact diameter of the earth

Another astronomical feature is that the perimeter of the Pyramid's base is equal to the circumference of a circle whose diameter is also *twice* the vertical of the Pyramid. The circle's circumference is 36524 inches.

9131, the number of inches on a side, multiplied, by four the number of sides, equals 36524, inches. Also, 5831, the number of inches in the vertical, multiplied by two to get the diameter of a circle, and then multiplied by 3.14159 to get the circumference, equals 36524.12534. (Fig. 75.)

The number is peculiar, for if the decimal be placed two points to the left it represents the number of days and fraction of a day required for one complete revolution of the earth about the sun=a year. The fraction is not exact, but a correction of one-tenth of an inch in the base side, or the diameter of the circle, (one-tenth of an inch in about 10000 inches) would remedy the defect—and we are not that certain of the measurements given. The subject of days will come hereafter.

The above two problems show the importance, in Pyramid measurements, of the circle whose radius is equal to the height of the Pyramid. The diameter of this circle into the earth-sun distance equals the earth's diameter. The circumference equals the number of days in a year with the decimal point placed two degrees to the right.

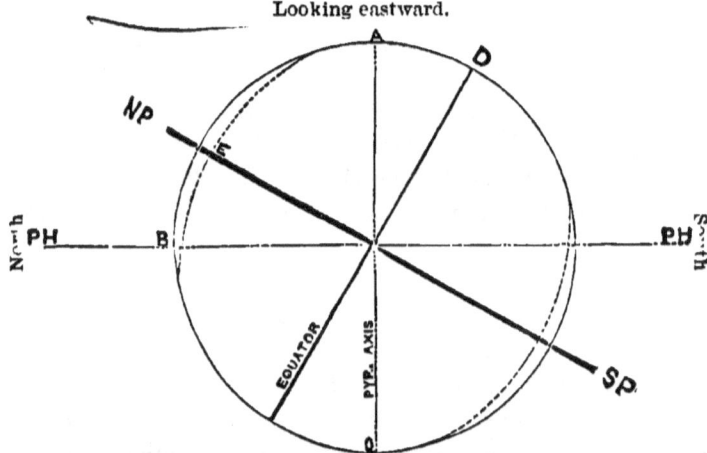

Fig. 74. A, Pyramid. D, Equator. N P, North Pole. S P, South Pole. P H, Plane of the Heavens, the polar axis being inclined 30°.

Under the head of astronomical relations come many singular cosmical facts. For instance, the Pyramid is placed on a certain parallel of latitude, and being there, is, of itself, sufficient evidence that it was so placed by design. A line drawn through the Great Pyramid, around the earth, parallel to the Equator, will divide the land surface of the globe into two equal sections. It will be that parallel which covers more land surface than any other line which can be drawn. However slight this circumstance may appear at first glance, under the light of the other mathematical relations, and a fragment of history which has descended to us, it becomes the most important fact ever chronicled in the history of science, and may lead yet to most important discoveries. It is folly to intimate that the ancients, in general, understood the size and shape of earth. The common people certainly did not. All written testimony, and all inscribed science, teaches the belief in flat surfaces, *or* imaginary supports for the earth. But farther still, how could they have known of the vast territory of Australia and Australasia? Or the great Continent of America? Yet not only does the Pyramid's exact location monumentalize the existence of continents, but it "weighs them in the balances" of some Almighty power—grander than instinct, more sublime than human intellect, more technical and intricate than coincidence or clairvoyance!

But some doubting one may suggest: "It was erected in Egypt; Ghizeh offered a suitable spot; it was coincidence—not that the Pyramid was built there,—but that the *Egyptians* were there!" True, if the Pyramid *were* built by the Egyptians, and were shorn of all these wonders except such as an ignorant but warlike people could have produced. But the *other* wonders *are* there, and this is with them; and no historian can consistently state, although he may deem it possible, that the Egyptians built it. A wonderful testimony is given by Josephus, a writer who had the most intimate acquaintance with the pre-Hebraic theosophic history of any ancient writer. He makes an untrimmed assertion that the God fearing son's of Seth, seeing the knowledge which came to them from a divine source, dying out, built two monuments—one of brick and one of stone.* This stone monument was to contain the science of the universe. And of course, they built it at home where they could best labor and study—in Chaldea! Not so. For from some impulse—or guidance—or scientific knowledge, they went to that point on the earth's surface where it alone could unlock these mysteries of cosmos—to the "Siriad," or Egypt. Nor could they have selected a less likely location from a human standpoint—for at that time Chaldea and Palestine were the Garden of the world, while Egypt was an oasis, peopled by descendants of Ham, the banished one—a race cursed in the Bible by terrible prophecies which have been fulfilled to the very letter. Put this statement of Josephus by the side of the tradition of Melchizedek and Philitis, and the history of Heroditus, and then ask, Who built the Pyramid? A foreign, or a native race?

But to secure that parallel which divided the earth's land surface in halves was not the only object in building the monument in Egypt. As will be shown hereafter, the shape of the Pyramid gives us the quadrature of the circle. To do this required a certain shape and certain construction, and that construction produced a certain Azimuthal indication of latitude. That indication was for the 30th parallel—the only parallel on the globe where the geometrical and astronomical relations would harmonize!

---

* "They were the inventors of the peculiar sort of wisdom which is concerned with the heavenly bodies and their order. And as Adm predicted that the world was to be destroyed at one time by water, and another time by fire, they made two pillars, one of brick, and another of stone, so that if the brick pillar was [were] destroyed, the stone might remain and exhibit their discoveries to mankind. Now this stone pillar remains in the land of Siriad (Egypt) to this day."—(Josephus' Antiquities, Book 1, Sec. 2 and 3.)

ASTRONOMY. 131

We have not the space to work out this problem, but it indicates a God-like intelligence to have originally conceived it. The latitude of the Pyramid is now given as 29°56'6", involving a possible error of 54" in the 1,296,-000" in the earth's circumference—possibly due to our faulty instrumentation, or possibly an azimuthal change in polar axis during 5,000 years. It will be farther noticed that the Pyramid axis (Fig.74) is about 90° from the Plane of the Heavens. Now we know the earth to be spheroidal in shape. Hence, is not the circumferential difference from A to B less than O to B? Therefore, would 30° of latitude from the equatorial axis, on the earth's su f.ce represent 90° from the Plane of the

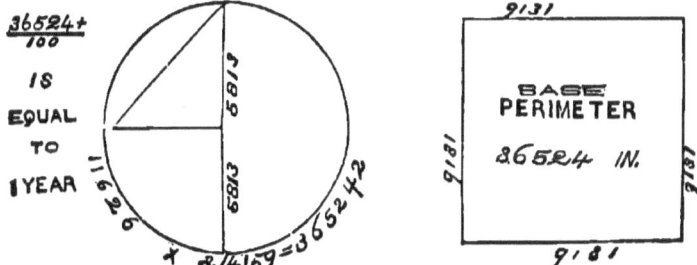

Fig. 75-6. Quadrature of the circle having the Pyramid-height for a radius, and the perimeter of the base, both equalling 100 years.

Heavens? We put the proposition plainly—that the 56" of deviation of the Pyramid's latitude from 30° is neither an error of inst umentation, nor a change in polar axis, but represents the spheroidal shape of the *earth!*

The Great Pyramid gives an approximate measurement of the earth's size in two ways. (The word "approximate" signifies fallibility in our measurements). 1st, by *breadth:* A band around the earth, the breadth of the Pyramid base, contains 100,000,000,000 square feet. The diameter*of

---
*By a Pyramid *Pi* calculation.

such a band is 500,946,700 inches. 2nd, by height: The height of the Pyramid multiplied by 270,000, divided by 3.14159 to get diameter, gives us very nearly even 500,000,000 inches, which is the polar diameter. The reason it is multiplied by 270,000 is that a circle equal to the area of the square base is 270,000 inches in circumference. It is plain that a mind who could provide for such vast mensuration understood the shape of the earth.

Our space will not permit following the astronomical and cosmical features farther; but the mine is scarcely opened; while if the key to the Great Monument were in our possession, these disconnected items would doubtless take proper and harmonious place in a complete and reasonable whole.

ORIENTATION.—The almost astronomically exact orientation of the Great Pyramid is indeed a remarkable feature. Without knowledge of the earth's shape, or motions, and an exact line from Alcyone to Draconis, the east-and-west, or north-and-south direction of the sides could not have been accomplished. It never did occur in other ancient buildings. Glidden remarks that this feature indicates that they were familiar with the compass, but it is known that the needle always points several degrees west of the direct north pole. The sun's rising would have been of no avail, for it varied from equinox to equinox. Altogether, the placing the structure east and west correctly is corroboration of the astronomical date of the Pyramid's erection.

The polar axis of the earth is generally accepted as 500,000,000 Pyramid inches. Twice the height of the Pyramid in inches (5813) equals 11626, or just 100 times the length of the ante-chamber. Now multiply the polar diameter by this, and reduce to miles, and we have 91,745,-

580 miles—very nearly the distance of the Sun, and agreeing with a strong report of a section of the observers of the recent transit of Venus.

THE METRICAL SYSTEM.

All of our readers are doubtless aware that the French Government seek the universal adoption of their metrical system for weights and measures. That is, that weights and measures should increase and decrease by a scale of 10, having the 1-ten-millionth part of the earth's polar quadrant for a standard. (Fig. 77.) This was called a "meter."

The principle involved in a decimal system is a good one, but the radical adoption of a system which would overturn the weights and measures of centuries would prove a national calamity. And still, were it necessary to attain the actual benefits to make a sacrifice, the world at large would undertake it. When, however, a nation undertakes to thrust upon us a system which is based upon acknowledged error, and is removed from the practical workings of trade and commerce, it is better not to embrace it too precipitately.

The great difficulty in fixing unalterable weights and measures is to secure a standard which shall never vary—one which the heat and cold of climate, electric conditions, or human interferences cann t modify. Nations have preserved standards at their capitals, but they will corrode, or shrink, or suffer from intriguing politicians. The 1-1000th of an inch makes little difference in a foot, but in the earth's circumference it spans some 25 miles!

The French nation adopted as their standard one ten millionth of a quadrant of the earth's circumference on a meridian at Paris. The folly of thus deliberately taking these measurements for a standard which can not be mathematically operated was only equalled by the more desperate folly of the bloody banishment of all religion from her borders at that time—the revolution. The circumference of a circle can never be mathematically measured. The arc is not much better. But worse yet—an arc which describes one quarter of a spheroid. Even the effort to establish a standard on a *curved line* was unscientific. This new standard—one 10-millionth of the quadrant—called a meter, is 39.371 inches in length—that is, it would be if it *were correct!* As it is, it is two small by 1-3500th. They also had the misfortune in producing a cognate standard of density to get spurious metal mixed with the cube, and untold calculations based upon the mass are "out of line."

The Pyramid has a metric system of its own—one that can teach modern science much, and modern antiquarians more—for the metric system of this hoary headed monarch proves to be that standard which has come down to us—filtered through all nations—from the remotest of times. It takes its standard from a straight line, and one mathematically immoveable—the only one on or *in* earth. It is one-half the polar axis, or the radius of a polar circumference. The earth's polar diameter is reckoned at 500,500,000 English inches. One 500,000,000th of this calculation equals 1,001 of our inches. This immensely small difference is not due to variation in the Pyramid, but in 5000 years of wear and tear the "inch universal" has been modified that much. The inch is the great standard of the Pyramid, and under some title is the real standard of the Celtic, Saxon, Gothic, and possibly, Teutonic races. 25 Pyramid inches equal the sacred cubit of the Jews. This can now be considered a settled fact.

This cubit, which often appears in the construction of

the Pyramid, is the 1-ten-millionth of the earth's radius of revolution (half-axis), or straight line used by the Pyramid to establish the inch. It is a cubit of most remarkably ancient history, being known as that measure "given by Jehovah to the Jews" to build all the sacred appurtenances of worship, including the temple and contents.

In the Pyramid it occurs prominently as follows: It is the measure of the top of the great niche in the Queen's Chamber, (p. 106). In order to ascertain the number of days in a year the base line is divided by that number which is a factor with 365.242,—the cubit of 25 inches. The embossing on the granite portcullis in antechamber, is supposed to be a cubit divided by five, being five inches long. Its height from the granite leaf is one-fifth of its breadth or just one-inch.

The length of the King's Chamber is 412.132 inches. Now 412.132 cubits is the diameter of a circle whose area equals the square base of the Pyramid—365.242 cubits on a side; and, on the other hand, a square having 412.132 cubits on a side is of equal area to a circle whose radius is equal to the height of the Pyramid, 232.520 cubits. Does any one imagine that these relations, which can be greatly extended—correct to a fraction—could occur if the sacred cubit were not involved in the construction?

It may be of note that not only is the sacred cubit employed, and the inch which has come down to us from a remote antiquity, but the coffer in the King's Chamber is of exactly the same cubical capacity of the "Ark of the Covenant," of the Hebrews. This coffer is a most wonderful object. It is the *great standard*, of which the modern British *Quarter* measure is just one-fourth! English people who measure a *quarter* of wheat do not realize that their "whole" measure is in the Pyramid! Is there any *chance* in the construction of this coffer? Its internal space has precisely the same cubical volume as its solid sides and bottom; the length of its sides constitute the circumference of a circle, the diameter of which is its height; it is just "one-fiftieth" the size of the chamber in which it is enclosed! The identity in capacity with the Ark of the Covenant (Tabernacle and Temple) confirms the theory of the use of the "sacred" cubit. The cubits of Memphis, Palestine, Babylon, Greece, etc., were very different measures. No other building in Egypt has been built by the sacred standard. Dr. Seiss emphasizes

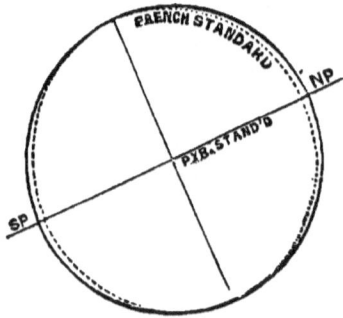

Fig. 77. Measure standards. N P, North Pole. S P, South Pole. Page 138.

Fig. 78. Relief sculpture on the granite bar or portcullis in Antechamber.

the fact that Solomon's "molten sea," was 50 times the size of the ark, and hence just the size of the King's Chamber.

By these scattered evidences in the Pyramid, we know a certain system of linear measure has pervaded the social and commercial fabric since the human race originated. The inch has been referred back to the "thumb-breadth." Inches make a palm and palms a cubit. But even the cubit may now be discovered in this structure which antedates history. So modern measurement appears to have as ancient an origin, the coffer agreeing precisely with the Anglo-Saxon quarter.

This ancient system being based on the only cosmical standard of value, the axis of the earth's rotation, why demoralize the commerce of the world to force upon the people a system whose linear is in error by computation, and whose metallic standard is in error by adulteration?

S.ill worse were such a policy when it is exceedingly unpractical to "jump" measures by multiples of 10. Inasfar as the decimal system can be fairly used the Pyramid system contains it. A decimal scale to be of use must break up into convenient fractions. Our money is only partially decimal. The half-dime, quarter-dollar, 3-cent-piece, quarter eagle, etc., illustrate this. The foot of 12 inches may be changed to 10. But the inch can never be taken away. And with the foot of 10 inches, what more natural division next than the quarter of a hundred, "25," —a cubit. Then 100 cubits now equal an "acre-side." In weight measure the great scientific standard for mean specific gravity, is exactly the 1-2500th part of the cubical contents of the coffer, and give us the modern "pint"— a Pyramid pound, as it is "the world around." This pound divides evenly by 10 for grains, and increases by decimal multiples and four for chaldrons, tons, etc. Then if the national standard must be simplified let it be by those slight changes which will conform it to the great standard which has remained imperishable since the foundation of society.

Before passing this topic we add a few problems from a pamphlet just sent us by its Author, an accomplished Civil Engineer,[*] showing the relation of the cubit to the

[*] "The French Metric System, or The Battle of the Standards," by Chas. Latimer, Cleveland, Ohio. For sale by C. H. Jones & Co., 188 Monroe St., Chicago.

Pyramid: The total length of the Antechamber floor is 116.26 inches. It is the diameter of a circle whose circumference is 365.242=to the days in a year; multiplied by a cubit it equals 9131 inches, the base side of the Pyramid

This 116.26 multiplied by 50, (a double cubit, and course of masonry on which the Antechamber rests), we have the vertical of Pyramid, 5813 inches. But 116.26 multiplied by 2=the vertical in cubits.

The granite floor of the Antechamber is 103.033 inches long. It goes into the breadth of the King's Chamber twice exactly, its length 4 times, and its height 2.236 times—which latter figure is the square root of five. The sum of the squares of these numbers (4, 16, and 5) is 25= to the sacred cubit. Into the diagonal of the end of the King's Chamber this 103.033 will go 3 times; into the floor diagonal 4.472 times, into the side diagonal 4.582 times. The sum of the squares of these numbers is the double cubit, 50.

The length of the King's Chamber, 412.132 inches is the diameter, in cubits, of a circle whose area is equal to a square the size of the base of the Pyramid.

A square having 412.132 cubits for the length of a side is equal in area to a circle whose radius is equal to the Pyramid's height.

QUADRATURE OF THE CIRCLE

The real mathematical problem involved in the construction of the Great Pyramid is not yet evolved. The chronological analogies, and the astronomical features, are only disconnected wonders which indicate the presence of a precise and consistent plan upon which the whole structure was erected. Angulation and mensuration, section, the properties of the circle, square, triangle, elipsis, and parabola; the cognate forms of sphere, cube, pyramid, spheroid, and cone, were apparently understood and manipulated by the designer. The astronomical elements may extend far beyond our present comprehension, as we only stand upon the threshold with a few of the plainer problems in hand.

It is among the most remarkable circumstances, that the first discovery of profound mathematical import in the Pyramid was the sudden interpretation of what is known as the π proposition, (Greek letter Pi). This is the substance of the quadrature of the circle, represented by the formula:

Diameter : Circumference :: 1 : 3.14159+ or Pi.

The formula is the nearest means of finding the side of a square which is of equal area to a circle. The exact operation which will reduce a circle to a square of equal area has never been found.

The Quadrature of the Circle, is one of the great problems associated with mathematics in all ages. It is not, as some have supposed, in recent Pyramid literature, the reduction of a circle to a square form of *equal perimeter*, but its reduction to a square of equal area. The circle is a polygon, with an infinite number of sides, and mathematics can never measure a curved line any nearer than to compute for a number of sides to any circle until they are so small that the error is unimportant. Hence, the relation of a circle to a square is the computation of the area of a polygon; but this polygon has an unlimited number of sides. The formula for computation may be (1) to multiply the square of the radius by the proportion of the diameter to the circumference, or (2) multiply the radius by the circumference for a rectangle, and the square root of the half of it will give one side of a square of equal area to the circle. Both of these formulæ require the circumference, or the proportion of circumference to the diameter. Therefore, the great difficulty in the way is to secure this proportion. And in mathematics it is always known as the *Pi* proposition.

Archimedes proved that the relation of the diameter to the circumference was nearly that of 1 to $3\tfrac{10}{71}$ using a polygon of 96 sides. Ludolph Von Ceulen computed a circle having 36,893,488,147,419,103,232 sides, and the fraction he secured thereby was—(D=diameter; C= x or circumference):

D : C :: 1 : 3.1415926535897932384626433832795 0288+.

The error in this computation is so small that in a circle whose radius is 250,000 times the distance of the earth from the sun, the correction would be less than the millionth of the width of a human hair.

Does the Pyramid represent this *Pi* proposition? It does. Do other Egyptian monuments represent it? No, not one. Could not this peculiar shape be a coincidence? *Once* among a thousand million chances, but not a dozen times in one monument!

Fig. 79 represents the two prominent problems involved. The square ABCD is the base, 9131.05 on a side. E to F is the vertical height. The vertical is to twice the base side as 1 is to *Pi:*

5813 : 9131.05×2 :: 1 : 3.14159+.

This is a very singular fact. But the perimeter of the square base is also equal to the circumference of the circle— Diameter of circle being 11626 :

$$9131.05 \times 4 = 36524.2$$
$$11626 \times 3.14159 = 36524.2.$$

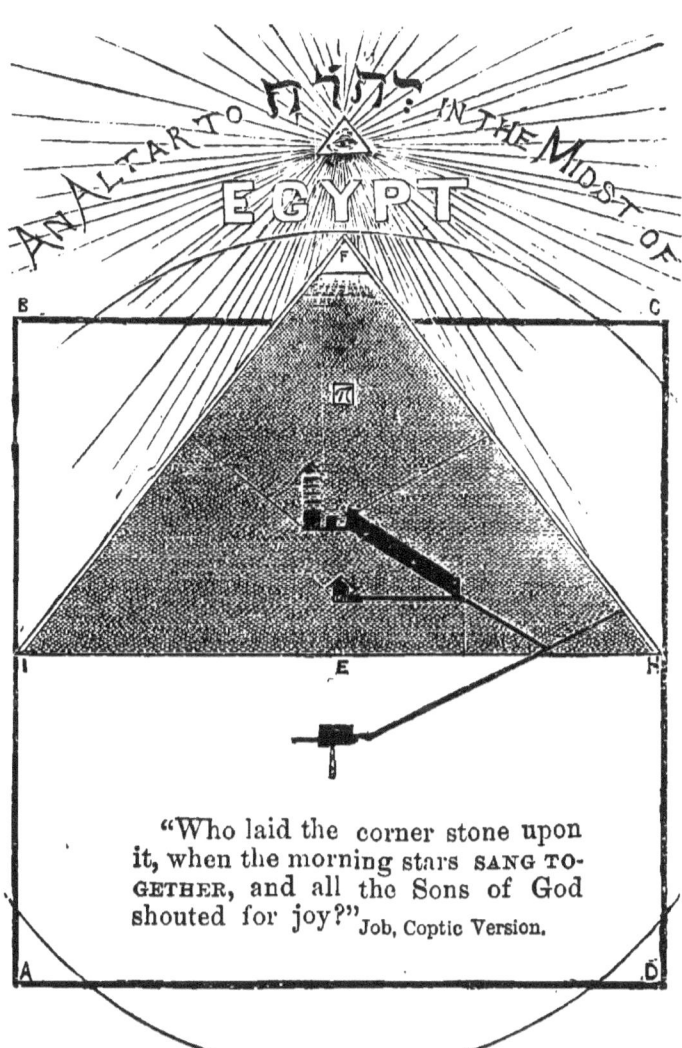

Fig. 79.

Is there any thing remarkable about this? Does not 36524.2 equal 100 years to an hour? There are exactly 365.242 days in a year, and the decimal system, with a moveable point, is used all through the Pyramid. *Why*, we hope to find hereafter. Again, the diameter of 11626 bears the same relation to the length of the Antechamber, which is 116.26 long. Thus the base gives us a *Pi* proportion; the vertical gives it, and now the Antechamber does the same. Let us examine the King's Chamber. It is 412.132 inches long. The area of a circle of equal diameter, squared, gives the Pyramid's base. Again, the circuit of the side wall, (all the granite, that may dip below the floor) divided by 412.132=*Pi*. There are other illustrations in the Antechamber. The number of cubic inches in the granite bar, or portcullis, across Antechamber is *Pi* muliplied by 10,000. The Queen's Chamber is crowded full of *Pi* proportions. The exact outer end of the entrance passage is computed by a *Pi* proportion. Then there is the Coffer! The measure standard for the world! Its height is to the side and end as 1 is to *Pi*. In fact 3.14159 seems to be impressed all over the structure. A circle, with the breadth of the coffer's base for diameter, or a square with the depth of the coffer, equal the area of a side divided by *Pi*.*

Why, we ask, is it that this ever present Quadrature proportion is so intimately connected with the *days in a year?* Is it possible that the great mystery of the Quadrature is symbolized in a day? That the greatest circumferen c known to the earth—being infinitely incommensurable, like all other circles—is thus crystalized in the lesser circle of revolution? For if the revolution of the earth around the sun can never be exactly measured, can

*"Miracle in Stone."

a day? Is not *this* the secret of our faulty cycle, and does not that Pyramid, which embodies the Great Precessional Cycle of the Heavens, also concrete the infinitude of *time* into its mass, by these ever-recurring symbols of an infinite fraction? Even the great precessional circle is a *Pi* proportion—does the Pyramid really contain its exact circumference? It is our hope, that when the Key is found to unlock the VAST MYSTERY which is tomb-shrouded in that sombre pile, the solution of Time's infinitude will appear in the wonderful revelation of complete proportion—in the Universe of God. Nor do we believe the many laborious but unhappy souls who are figuring on the Quadrature of the Circle, Perpetual Motion, Trisection of the Triangle, etc., will ever enter their Aden until the Lethe of the Pyramid is bridged, and the "Stars shout for joy!"

All studies of Physics involve certain conditions to secure accuracy. Among these, is an unalterable temperature; and absolute unchangeableness of the humidity of the atmosphere, and positive rest. Thus, mass attraction, or specific gravity, can only approximately be obtained from want of these conditions. Deep cellars and vaults have been constructed in which to experiment. Standards of measure have surely suffered from these causes. Metal standards will expand and shrink with the slightest variation of temperature. Micrometer scales detect it, and also delicate pyrometers. And a difference of a thousandth of an inch in one yard, will displace rivers, and mountains, and planets, in vast calculations.

Near the Pyramid center, where rests the Coffer, the apparent standard of measure and gravity, the temperature never varies. The humidity is invariable. 180 feet of masonry protect it in the nearest approach to the surface. And if the King's Chamber varies any, the Subterranean Chamber is as silent and unalterable as the womb of earth itself. In the midst of the mystery of the Pyramid is this provision for the perfect preservation of standards for future measures. The temperature is 68° F.

TIME DIVISIONS.

As already illustrated, the Great Cycle of time measured by the precession of the equinoxes, or revolution of the heavens, ·25,826.68 years in extent, is so prominently recorded in the Pyramid that no doubt of *intention*, on the part of the builder, can be entertained. It constitutes, also, indisputable evidence (to our mind) that the period of its erection was 2170 B. C., the beginning of the Great Cycle.

The year is also represented in centuries, as given in the numerous problems of the previous sections. The most prominent, is the fact that the perimeter of the base of the Pyramid represents a century, each side being 25 years in extent. Thus 9131.05 inches divided by the sacred cubit (25 inches) equals 365.242, or one year, even to the hours, minutes, and seconds. The century is also given by the circle which has the height for a radius, (Fig. 75). In this we have the measurement of time represented as an incommensurable—produced by multiplication with 3.14159, or *Pi*.

The Grand Gallery is given by some, however, as a symbol of the divisions of the year.

And the first prominent indication is for weeks. The various considerations presented to us have led us to believe the Grand Gallery especially devoted to "Time," and hence its peculiarities may well be referred to time divisions. Therefore it is said that the seven overlapping stones, or tiers of masonry in the sides represent the weeks of seven days. Ten and five are the Pyramid numbers, seven rarely entering as a factor. However, the Grand Gallery is seven times as high as its entrance passage. That part of the horizontal passage in the "cut away" of Grand Gallery floor, (Fig. 53, p. 87), is one-seventh the whole length of the horizontal passage. The enlarged south end of the horizontal passage is also one-seventh of the entire length. The Queen's Chamber has seven sides. Mr. Smyth refers all these circumstances, as symbols, to the week of seven days. We do not see any application except in the case, possibly, of the overlapping stones of the Grand Gallery. It is difficult to see why the passage should be so low and difficult, and the Grand Gallery suddenly seven times higher without some symbolical import. Prof. Smyth likewise held the idea that the seven overlapping tiers on each side represented *two weeks* of months, or 14 months of 26 *days* to the year. And this he regarded as a more reasonable division than 12 months, as it leaves but one day to be added to 26 days at the end of the year, and two on leap years. At present we add five or six days to one-twelfth of 360, or 30, the even length of our months. Then to indicate the imperfections of the months there are 28 ramp holes on one side and 26 on the other; and the two last—at upper end of Grand Gallery, extend under the wall, as if referring the observer to the Antechamber. In the Antechamber we find on the sides four ridges; three curved, or hollowed, and one full and straight.

These are supposed to represent the three imperfect years, and the fourth perfect. Some other refinements are added to this theory. On the whole, while it may contain the germs of a great truth, the evidences lack strength, and do not satisfy a dem nstration by considerable.

THE STONE LOGOS.

The most remarkable development of the G.eat Pyramid is its relation to that religion which has descended to us through the Abrahamic race. Of course this relation is not susceptible of "proof," but is capable of a very general elaboration.

A just judgment of the value of the Biblical references and relations requires more than a passing knowledge of the language employed in the Bible. It must give not a little weight to the history of those races descended from Shem, but out of the Abrahamic succession; for, no doubt, the Caphtorim, the Canaanites in general, and the races under the mysterious Melchizedek, were part of the original monotheists. The peculiar history of the Pyramid's erection ; its freedom from idolatrous hieroglyphs, present in every other tomb and temple in Egypt, and its marvelous problems—almost if not quite prophetic—also should be taken into account. Again, the *order* of the events related to each other, chronologically, deserve the careful consideration of the student:—The Flood, the settlement of Canaan and Egypt, the lives of the patriarchs, the origin of letters, the migration of Jacob's children and their Exodus,—the building, sealing and discovery of interior of the Pyramid—all make up a history in which there is a common theme and an identical theism. The prophetic nature of the chronology, contained in the passages, representing events in the history of the Hebrew race, is a strong indication of a theistic design on the part of the builder. The peculiar prominence of the "sacred cubit" is also worthy of notice, especially as this cubit (25 Pyramid inches) was not in use either by the Egyptians or Hebrews as a people. It was given of God, as witnessed by Ezekiel (Chap. xl), and consisted of a "cubit and a hand breadth."* That this cubit is also the earth's semi-axis divided by 10^7 as represented by Herschel, is also a wonderful fact. The striking analogy in size and cubical contents between the King's Chamber and the "H ly of Holies" in the Temple, has been pointed out to us, but the analogy may not be direct and close enough to indicate an intention to duplicate the one in the other.

The probable size (cubic contents), of the ark of the covenant presents a very striking analogy. The exterior of the ark, as given in the Bible, in inches, was 62.5 inches long, 37.5 wide, and 37.5 deep. Now allowing for the probable width of the sides and bottom and we have a mean of 71,247.5 cubic inches as the probable capacity, which corresponds with great exactness to the mean coffer capacity. It would also appear that four omers, or measures of fluid, equalled one ark of dry measure, being thus parallel to the British quarter. Added to the many physical s'gns which point to a relation between the Pyramid and the theosophic history of the Hebrews, we find many references which point directly to this monument.

Many parts of the Book of Job are supposed to refer to it, but to our mind not distinctly enough, unless the relation of a divine builder be established by other evidences. The most direct and incontrovertable reference is in the 19th Chapter of Isaiah, 19-20th verses: "In that day shall there be an altar to the Lord in the *midst* of the Land of Egypt, and a pillar at the border thereof, to the Lord. And it shall be for a sign, and for a witness unto the Lord of Hosts in the Land of Egypt."

---

*The irregular cubit of the ancients varied—in the neighborhood of 20 inches.

It will be remembered, in reading this, that in Isaiah's time there was no admiration on the part of the Jews, for the land of Egypt—that each prophet in succession had poured out vials of bitter prophetic denunciation against the Nile Valley, all of which have been most wonderfully fulfilled. It will be well, also, to bear in mind, that that very portion of the Pyramid, which represents the Jews shows them as a "cut off" from the ascending passage, and enlarged Grand Gallery, plodding along painfully, in a narrow, rough, unfinished passage, whose very mortar was mixed with *salt,*(*vide* Jewish customs, and the salting of the earth at destruction of Jerusalem).

Is there any "pillar," or "altar," in Egypt to which this significant expression can refer? Egypt is free from monotheistic monuments other than this stalwart prophet of stone. Is there any interpretation to the words: "In that day," applicable to the Pyramid? Singularly enough this witness was sealed from the world for twenty-five centuries after Isaiah's time, and its mysteries are only now becoming dimly visible in theistic and cosmic sense, in this dawn of that prophetic promise of millenial glories.

Admitting these peculiarities, is there any construction of the language employed which gives topographical evidence that the Great Pyramid was to be God's Witness? Prophecy sits upon the ruins of Babylon, Tyre, Edom and Egypt, and from the Euphratean marshes to the sands which carnival in and out of Petrea's cliff-palaces—not a frown of the Almighty has been wasted. What then of this witness? Two thousand years before Christ, Memphis stood near the seashore, and the Memphian pyramids were on the border of the encroaching sands. To-day there is a plain stretching out from ancient Egypt into the sea, which harmonizes two antithetic phrases in Isaiah's prophecy: *In the midst of Egypt, and yet in the border thereof.*

The meaning of this was a mystery until cleared up by one of those Providences which come from indirect agencies. A United States naval officer, in passing the coast of Egypt noticed that the shore line constituted an arc of a circle, the converging radii of which meet at the hill of Ghizeh. This idea did not originate in any desire to develop Pyramidology. A carefully prepared map illustrated the fact very strongly, an imitation of which appears on page 151.

At present, taking the geometrical shape of the valley as a guide, the Great Pyramid of Ghizeh is in the center of a circle, whose circumference bounds the extremities. At the same time it is upon the border thereof. Westward stretches the dreary waste of sand. Eastward the fertile valley. It is also on the border which separated Upper from Lower Egypt. No language could have been used by man so appropriately to mark its situation —nor could more foolish words be spoken than these, provided the Great Pyramid were not intended.

The following extract from Job is doubtless the most direct of any that has been appropriated to the Pyramid —the Lord answering Job out of the whirlwind:

"Who is this that darkeneth counsel by words without knowledge? Gird up now thy loins, like a man, for I will demand of thee, and answer thou me, where wast thou when I laid the foundations of the earth?* Declare if thou hast understanding. Who laid the measures thereof, if thou knowest? Or who hath stretched the line upon it? Whereupon are the foundations fastened ["made

---

*If the sides of the Pyramid are continued through the earth at the same ratio of 10 to 9, the intersection of the axis of revolution will be at the poles. (Extract from a recent work—but an error.)

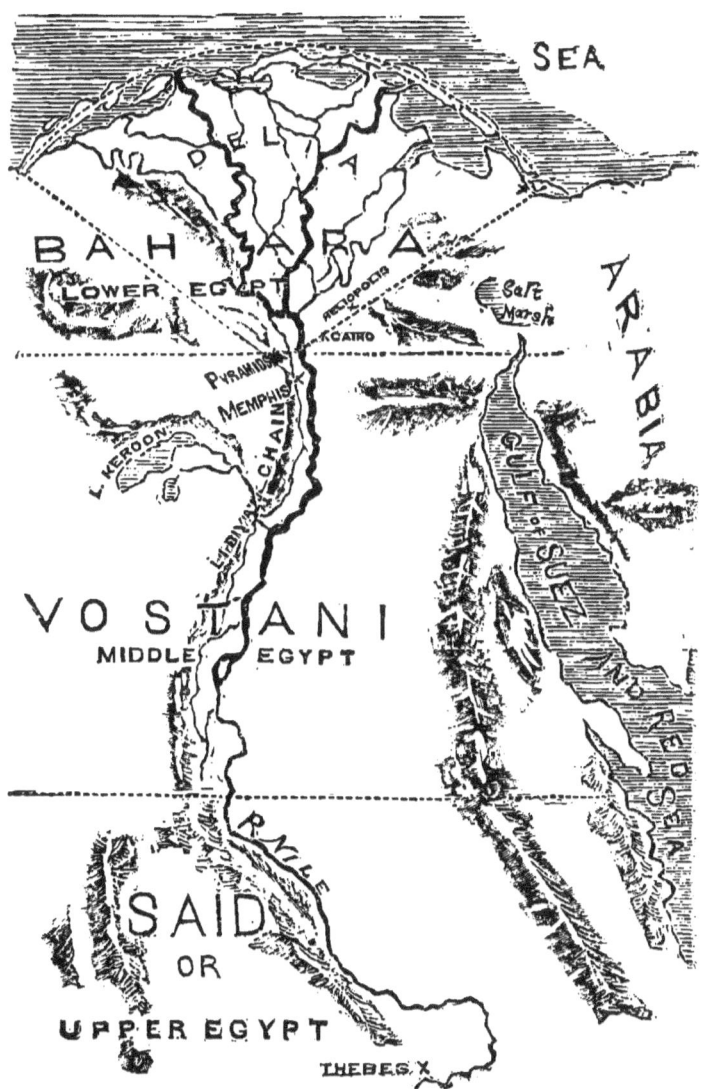

Fig. 80. Map with sector of a circle having the Pyramid as a centre.

to sink"].† Or who laid the corner stone thereof,‡ when the morning stars *sang together*, and all the Sons of God shouted for Joy?"

This is certainly a masterpiece of eloquence and power —yet so simple that a child can comprehend its majestic import. It will be noticed that the description of the foundations and erection of a structure are separated from and *precede* the reference to a corner stone. This occurs in the last sentence, one stone only being spoken of, and that, by liberal rendering, *upon* the structure, and when? When the morning stars sang together. Possibly this may refer to the unison of *a* Draconis and Alcyone at the grand "morning" of the great cycle—the Pleiadic year? How could the poetic expression of the beginning of the great year of the universe of God be more lofty and sublime than by the beautiful word "dawn"?—the "morning stars;" and the "corner stone" became more intelligible by a farther study of these expressions in the Bible. The Birth of Christ was signalled by a star, and referred to as a morning star, and throughout the entire written logos he is spoken of as a "corner stone." So pertinent are these references, that the missing corner-stone of this "stone logos"—in the wilderness—seems to be a symbol of the Christ,—who was welcomed with the *songs of angels*, but who has since been crucified and removed from earth.

We would also advise our readers to peruse Zechariah, 4th chapter, keeping the imagery of the building, the headstone, the mountain, and the expression of a "base," well in mind. Especially note the expression—"he shall

---

†Dr. Seiss.
‡The ancient Coptic Version has it "Who has laid the corner stone UPON

Fig. 81. Pyramids as seen from Old Cairo.

bring forth the headstone thereof with shoutings. Grace, Grace unto it." It is possible, as witnessed by what has been said, that the Great Pyramid is the prophetic symbol of the Church, the Temple, and the Logos, the Capstone being Jesus Christ, who is slain, whose birth was with song, and whose future advent, together with the discovery of the missing corner stone will be with shouts and songs of joy by God's people.

David says, "The stone which the builders refused has become the headstone of the corner."* In parallel words it is said in Acts 4 : 11, "This is the stone which was set at naught by you builde s, which has become the head of the corner." Read also 1st Peter, 2d chapter, from the 4th to the 8th verses, and note the distinctness of the expression of a "chief-corner stone." Especially the comparison of the Christian sect to a stone temple having a chief-corner stone in Christ Jesus, in Eph. 2:20-22. Follow this with the denunciations in Matthew 21: 42-44.

We must admit, after a careful consideration of this branch of Pyramid study, that the evidence of theistic teaching in the Pyramid analogous to the Hebraic theology, and referred to in the Hebrew writings, is more than enough to awaken the profoundest investigation of modern students. And yet, until the Pyramid presents more than fragmentary marvels, the connection with the great stream of theosophy must be seen as "through a glass darkly." That the unveiling of the marvellous structure will show that God's will, purpose, and agency is intertwined with its scientific attributes, we have no doubt. Such grand design, such depth of research, such intellectual grandeur, such harmony in execution, such wonderful prescience were never united in the "living" rock, except God fashioned its "corner-stone."

UNITED STATES SEAL.

In the early days of the republic, when the founders of the nation worked out the essentials of a government, they established a "seal." On one side was the Eagle, with the scutcheons and emblems representing the thirteen

---

*The Septuaginta say—"the head corner stone." It should be "head-corner stone"—compounding the two first words.

states, and various allegorical points we have not room to work out. On the reverse was placed a Pyramid, to represent strength, durability, and correctness of form. This was not a very singular choice, although the pyramids were then but slightly known.

Fig. 81. Reverse of U. S. Seal. There are different styles of this seal from the fact that it was never cut. The Act simply specified an unfinished pyramid, with addenda in the field.

But the directions require an *unfinished* Pyramid. This was a little singular. Then they added to it a "Radiant Eye," significant of the Watchcare of God over our people. Inasmuch as the missing corner stone is now universally recognized as symbolic of Jesus Christ, this selection of the complete design is still more remarkable.

OUR COINS.

In English inches the King's Chamber is 412.5 long; breadth is 206.2 inches. The silver "dollar of our Fathers" weighs 412.5 grains, the half-dollar 206.2 grains, and the quarter-dollar 102.1 grains, "which last is an important Pyramid number." The dollar was the weight of an eastern coin of traditional age, current in Asiatic trade, and ours was made to correspond.

The Pyramid height, in sacred cubits is 232.5. The gold eagle weighs 232.2 grains.

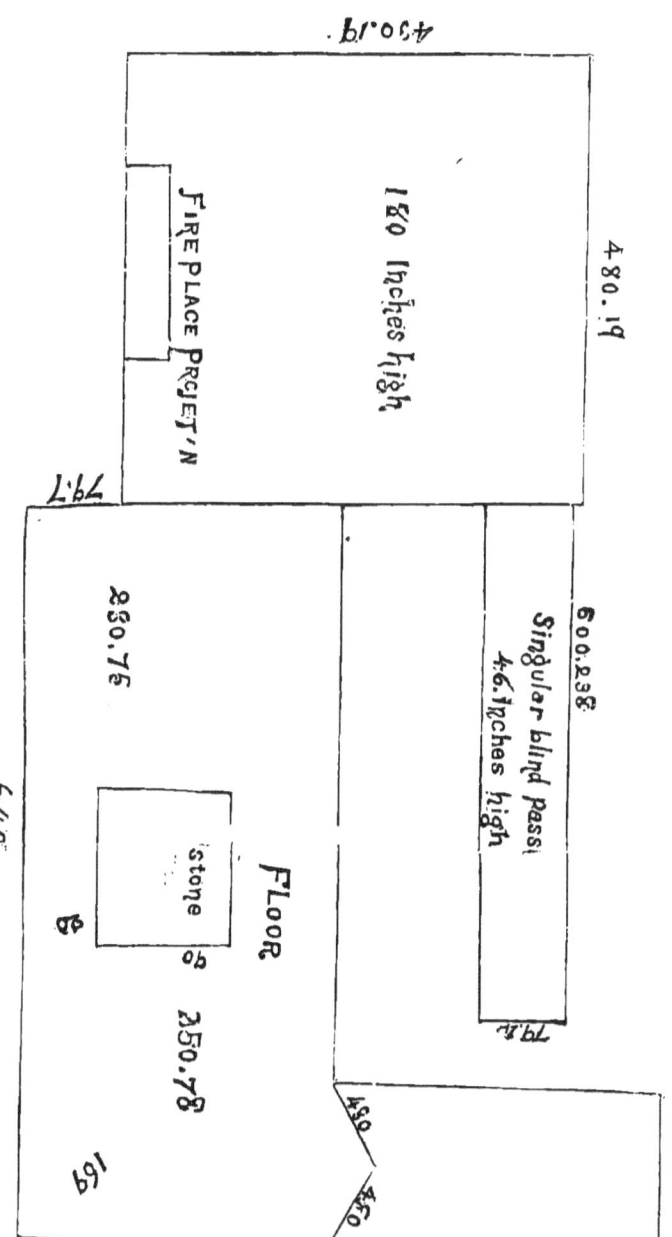

Fig. 83.

www.ingramcontent.com/pod-product-compliance
Lightning Source LLC
Chambersburg PA
CBHW030334170426
43202CB00010B/1125